GUIDED *by* *the* MOON

ALSO BY
Johanna Paungger and Thomas Poppe

Moon Time

THE WAXING AND WANING OF THE MOON

Waxing

first quarter

gibbous

crescent

2nd quarter

1st quarter

full moon

earth

new moon

3rd quarter

4th quarter

sunlight

gibbous

crescent

last quarter

Waning

JOHANNA PAUNGGER AND THOMAS POPPE

TRANSLATED FROM THE GERMAN BY DAVID PENDLEBURY

GUIDED
by *the* MOON

Living in Harmony
with the Lunar Cycles

· MARLOWE & COMPANY ·
NEW YORK

GUIDED BY THE MOON: *Living in Harmony with the Lunar Cycles*
Copyright © Johanna Paungger and Thomas Poppe 1996, 2000, 2002

Published by
Marlowe & Company
An Imprint of Avalon Publishing Group Incorporated
161 William Street, 16th Floor
New York, NY 10038

Originally published as *Vom richtigen Zeitpunkt* by
Heinrich Hugendubel Verlag in Munich, Germany.
This edition published by arrangement with
The C.W. Daniel Company Limited in England.

Library of Congress Control Number: 2002115209
ISBN 1-56924-502-9

9 8 7 6 5 4 3 2 1

DESIGNED BY PAULINE NEUWIRTH, NEUWIRTH & ASSOCIATES, INC.

Printed in the United States of America
Distributed by Publishers Group West

Contents

☽

CONTENTS

CONTENTS

Contents

Foreword to the American Edition

☾

FOR THOUSANDS OF years the knowledge of the influence of lunar rhythms has been an established tool that is available to all who are willing to accept it. Countless people in numerous occupational groups had used that knowledge as an indispensable element in their work—from physicians, farmers, and carpenters to architects, hairdressers, and foresters—until, for reasons we explore later in the book, this knowledge fell into disuse for several decades. Today we're pleased to say that many people all over the world have once again remembered this incalculably valuable inheritance of our forefathers. We are very happy that we are now able to pass this knowledge on to our readers in North America.

The Moon is inextricably linked to many aspects of our lives. Scores of gardeners, farmers, and most of all the multitude of indefatigable "balcony farmers" in the cities have experienced firsthand the great value of living in harmony with the lunar rhythms. They have seen that it's possible to forget pesticides and fertilizers and stop wasting valuable drinking water and still harvest the same or a higher yield at a much higher quality of crops and herbs. That's what true life-containing food is made of!

Practitioners, physicians, and dentists have seen how working in accordance with the position of the moon proved to be a blessing for their patients and have used this knowledge to explain a great many strange phenomena surrounding therapy and healing processes. Being skilled and well prepared is essential, but our moon calendars are hanging openly on the walls of many medical offices and hospitals to help in choosing the best times for surgeries and therapeutic measures.

There isn't a single forester or carpenter in our home countries of Germany and Austria who hasn't heard of this book. They have seen that wood cut at the correct time is far more durable and the carpenters' work becomes more environmentally sound—inside and outside of the house. Wood is no longer corrupted by the poisonous varnishes or protective paints that cause health problems for the structure's inhabitants. It can remain what it is: The most beautiful and healthy building material nature gives us.

Hairdressers and beauticians have also observed with joy that the application of the moon rhythms is of good service in their professions and they are able to work without using many of their usual products, which contain excessive amounts of chemicals. Natural cosmetics thus get the chance it deserves.

Last but not least, housewives have received the knowledge of the art of moon timing with open arms. Millions today know firsthand what a great little household helper knowledge of the lunar cycles can be, and all that's required is a little patience! It is the housewives first and foremost who have denied that this knowledge is merely a fashionable trend. They have no need for scientific proof—when it comes to cleaning, half the work and twice the fun speaks for itself.

This book is ushering in a minor revolution. May the knowledge it contains bring you just as much usefulness and pleasure as it has brought to many people before you and to us.

Johanna Paungger-Poppe
Thomas Poppe

Foreword

☾

FOR MANY YEARS people have constantly been asking me to pass on a body of knowledge with which I grew up from my earliest childhood—the knowledge of lunar rhythms and the influences exerted on all forms of life on earth which are indicated by the position and phases of the moon. I have to thank my grandfather for teaching me that instinct, perception, and experience are the keys to many things in nature that science alone is unable to unveil.

I can still remember very well the first lecture I ever gave. People warned me that I would have to deal with derision. And yet my inner conviction was so firm, and I was so sure of the support of my friends, that I didn't care how many of the audience laughed at me. For me only one thing mattered: if even a single person received this natural and self-evident material, then it would keep alive an ancient knowledge maintained for centuries by virtue of being handed down, tested, and applied, and which especially at the present time could be of great value for us all and for the world in which we live.

The success of this first lecture encouraged me to give others; and now, after many such lectures, I am writing my experiences down. I am especially pleased at the openness that many people have shown toward the knowledge of lunar rhythms. If at first I saw many incredulous faces, there nonetheless developed an intense interest even after a very short time. Today many doctors and employers actually use "the guidance of the moon" in their professional work. For me there is absolutely nothing new about dealing with the phases of the moon, but I am happy that many people are once more placing their trust in this ancient knowledge. Even if you did not grow up, as I did, with this knowledge, you now have the opportunity to accumulate your own experiences, and that is a thousand times more useful than examples in a book.

This is my wish: that you may obtain, if you so desire, a knowledge that can accompany you throughout the whole of your life without having to be forever looking up textbooks, guides, and tables—a knowledge that becomes second nature to you and that you can pass on to your children as a springboard for their own experience.

This book was written in collaboration with Thomas Poppe. I hope that it may make life easier for every person of good will who reads it and that it may serve as a helpful companion in a great many of life's situations.

Johanna Paungger

Great adventures sometimes have trivial, unspectacular beginnings—for example the ringing of a telephone.

"Hey, I've just met this woman that you might find really interesting. Maybe you could write a book together. She's called Johanna Paungger. I told her about you and she wants to meet you . . ."

"Write a book? What about?" I answered, somewhat irritably, as I was in the middle of grappling with a book I didn't like, and my inspiration had deserted me.

"Wait and see: it's not so easy to explain."

That's all I needed.

Well, being inquisitive by nature, I agreed. I had no idea at the time what was heading my way.

Many events and experiences in my life deserve the description "extraordinary, strange, uplifting, enriching," but my meeting with Johanna Paungger does not fit into any of these categories. The quality of the encounter with her was so new to me that there were no standards available to me by which to measure it and place it in some corner or other of my thinking and feeling.

Not that anything unusual or sensational took place: we met in a forest café, spoke only sparingly about the subject of the proposed book, exchanged friendly remarks and anecdotes in order to surmount the initial distance between us, and philosophized about this and that. She said she had read one of my books and felt that I was the right person to work with her on writing an account of an ancient body of knowledge. She told me about her Tyrolean homeland, her childhood as one of ten children in a family of mountain farmers, how she had moved to Munich—and again and again, almost incidentally, she slipped in allusions to a special knowledge that was still widespread back home, and that her grandfather had communicated to her: the knowledge concerning the rhythms of the moon and their influence on nature, man, beast, and plant.

One anecdote that casts a light on her apprenticeship with her grandfather remains in my memory. She related that the long years of learning had gone by almost without anything being said—only watching, observing, grasping, experiencing. But one day she had actually asked a question: I believe it was in connection with gathering a particular medicinal herb. Her grandfather had answered, "Just watch really closely."

There were many further meetings with Johanna Paungger, and it was a long while before we finally sensed with certainty the time was ripe to start on a book. We had got to know one another and gained each other's trust. More and more people were coming to her lectures, beginning to show an interest in this ancient knowledge, and urging her to write everything down. This book is the outcome of a harmonious teamwork, a mutual cooperation that I can only describe as happy. Ms. Paungger contributed her knowledge and her experience and I provided my pen and my experience. From time to time, however, you will find short passages written in the first person that depict personal experiences and observations by Ms. Paungger or myself.

Even writing itself became a very special learning process for me. In the beginning I forgot the old proverb that "Enthusiasm for the learner is like sleep for the hunter." Gradually it became clear to me that Johanna Paungger doesn't want to prove anything and doesn't want to teach anybody—that knowledge has no need of any kind of justification, since it proves itself solely by means of itself. What matters most to her is to take away from the reader the conviction that he has found yet another patent remedy, perhaps even a panacea, with which to deal with all his problems. Even keeping to the "right moment" does not help in the long run if thought and attitude are not in harmony. A crutch, such as keeping to rules and laws, can actually only fulfill one purpose: one leans on it as long as it is necessary, and then one throws it away when it is no longer needed. This knowledge should become second nature and lead to alertness toward both oneself and the environment. Daily experience and experimentation with these rules sharpens our attention to the things that surround us and leads us to recognize the connections with our own lives, which ultimately go beyond the rules.

In olden times it was the noblest duty of a man of knowledge, whether craftsman or philosopher, to pass on his knowledge (not his hunches, assumptions, opinions, or convictions) in a responsible manner. Now for the first time the knowledge of lunar rhythms, insofar as this is definable in writing, is available to us together with an abundance of tips and advice dealing with almost all the important areas of our daily life from medicine to housekeeping and nutrition, to gardening and work on the land.

Patience is the only price you have to pay in order to profit by this book. Then it can really become a building block for another world.

Thomas Poppe

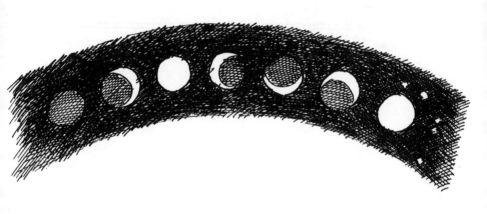

O N E

The Seven Impulses of the Moon

IT IS SO PLEASANT TO EXPLORE NATURE AND ONESELF AT THE SAME TIME,
DOING VIOLENCE NEITHER TO HER NOR TO ONE'S OWN SPIRIT,
BUT BRINGING BOTH INTO BALANCE IN GENTLE, MUTUAL INTERACTION.

—Goethe

PAST AND PRESENT

FOR THOUSANDS OF years man lived largely in harmony with the manifold rhythms of nature in order to ensure his survival. He observed with eyes wide open and bowed to necessity, at first without even asking about its causes. Eskimos, for example, live under some of the severest environmental conditions imaginable. Their language contains many different words for "snow," because they have learned to distinguish many different states of frozen water. The inhospitable climatic conditions compelled them to do so. Only two of these types of ice and snow are suitable for building the igloos they live in.

It was not just the state of things that human beings observed closely, but also the interrelationship between that state and the actual moment of observation—the time of day, month, and year, the position of the sun, moon, and stars. Many archaeologically significant buildings from ancient times testify to the importance our forefathers attached to the precise observation of heavenly bodies and the calculation of their paths. Nor was this just out of dispassionate scientific curiosity, but because these means helped them to derive the greatest possible benefits from knowing the prevailing influences of the current grouping of stars. The calendars that they worked out according to the course of the moon and the sun served to predict certain forces—impulses that only have an effect on nature, man, and beast at particular times and that recur at regular intervals. They were specifically able to particular those forces that, keeping pace with the course of the moon, exert an influence on all living things and are a contributory factor in the success or failure of hunt and harvest, storage, and healing.

Thus it was that the naturalist Charles Darwin in his classic work *The Descent of Man* only reported one of the discoveries that had been vouchsafed to countless generations before him and that had been of great benefit to them: "Man is subject, like other mammals, birds, and even insects, to that mysterious law, which causes certain normal processes, such as gestation, as well as the maturation and duration of various diseases, to follow lunar periods." Sharpened senses, alertness, perceptiveness, and exact observation of nature made our forefathers "masters of the art of lunar timing."

They discovered:

- ❧ that numerous natural phenomena—the tides, birth, meteorological events, women's menstrual cycle, and much more—are related to the movements of the moon
- ❧ that the behavior of many animals depends on the position of the moon; that birds, for example, always gather

their nest material at particular times, so that the nests dry
out rapidly after a rainfall

❧ that the effect and success of both countless everyday
activities and others that are less everyday—cutting
wood, cooking, eating, cutting hair, gardening, putting
down fertilizer, doing laundry, using medicines, perform-
ing surgical operations, and many other things—are subject to rhythms in nature

❧ that sometimes operations and doses of medicine administered on certain days can be helpful, while on other
days they can be useless or even harmful—often regardless of the amount and quality of the medication or the
skill of the doctor

❧ that plants and their component parts are exposed to
different energies from day to day—a knowledge of
which is crucial for successful cultivation, tending, and
harvesting of crops—and that herbs gathered at certain
times contain incomparably more active agents than at
others

In other words: the success of an intention depends not only on
the availability of the necessary skills and resources, but also deci-
sively on the timing of the action.

℃

OF COURSE OUR ancestors were at pains to pass on their knowledge and experience to their children. To do this it was necessary
to give the observed influences handy, easily understandable names,
and above all to couch them in a plausible overall system that
would enable the description of the forces and in particular the

prediction of future influences. A very special clock had to be invented.

The sun, moon, and stars naturally suggested themselves as an external framework—as the hands and dial, so to speak, of this clock—for a very simple reason: the essence of rhythm is repetition. If, for example, one observes that the most favorable time for sowing a particular plant lasts for exactly two to three days each month, and that the moon is always passing through the same stars at the time, then the idea occurs to group these stars into a "picture" and give the constellation a plausible name that typifies the quality of the influence in question. This constellation then becomes a figure on the clock face of the firmament.

In broad terms, our forefathers isolated 12 impulses, each possessing a different quality and coloring. To the stars through which the sun passes in the course of a year and the moon passes in the course of a month, they gave 12 different names.

Thus the twelve constellations of the zodiac came into being: Aries, Taurus, Gemini, Cancer, Leo, Virgo, Libra, Scorpio, Sagittarius, Capricorn, Aquarius, Pisces.

Man had created a star clock, from which he could read the influences that were prevailing at the moment and through which he could work out what helpful and hindering influences the future potentially held in store for his intentions. Many calendars in the past were based on the course of the moon because the forces indicated by the position of the moon in the zodiac are of far greater importance in our daily lives than the position of the sun. You are no doubt aware that even today many of our holidays depend on the position of the moon. Easter, for instance, since about the end of the second century A.D. has always been celebrated on the first Sunday after the first full moon of spring.

Toward the end of the nineteenth century the knowledge of these special rhythms of nature lapsed into oblivion almost overnight—perhaps also because any kind of systematization contains within it a sort of soporific drug. If my watch tells me it's twelve o'clock, there's no longer any need for me to observe the sun. When the direct perception of the impulses and forces governing a day is no longer taken into consideration, then the rules and laws rooted in this rapidly lose their force.

However, the main reason why this knowledge was abandoned is because modern technology and medicine promised us faster solutions for all the problems of daily life. Almost at a stroke, the observation of and respect for natural rhythms seemed to have become superfluous. Ultimately the knowledge lived on only in a few isolated areas.

The young farmers, foresters, and gardeners of modern times laughed at their parents and grandparents, spoke of superstition and began to rely almost entirely on the use of machines and instruments, fertilizers and pesticides. Thus they lost their contact with nature and began, at first unconsciously, to contribute to the destruction of the environment, always supported by an industry that understood how to maintain their confidence in its ability to solve every problem. Today there is hardly anyone left who can close his eyes to the high price that we have had to pay for disregarding the rhythms and laws of nature: yields are sinking and pests are having a field day because the soil is being exploited without being allowed to protect and regenerate itself; the use of pesticides has increased many times within a few decades without much appreciable success. The quality and health value of the harvested produce convey a very plain message.

The progress of the chemical and pharmaceutical industry has seduced the medical profession into the firm belief that they can disregard with impunity the cyclic flow and wholeness of life. The rapid removal of immediate pain and other overt symptoms was enough to count as "successful therapy"; research into root causes and slow-acting preventive measures and the patience and willingness for a long-term collaboration with the patient receded into the background. Moreover, using modern scientific methods, the knowledge of lunar rhythms may indeed be susceptible to proof, but scarcely to explanation; the question as to "why" must remain unanswered for the time being: in the linear thinking of most scientists this is a legitimate reason to ignore it altogether.

And all of us who so lightly turn our backs on the knowledge of these rhythms do so because on the one hand we have elevated short-term comfort to the highest good at the expense of reason and moderation. We believe we can outstrip everything, including nature, and in the process we outstrip ourselves. In the infernal tempo of our age we rush frantically from past to future. The present moment, the only point at which life actually occurs, is utterly lost.

> "The citizen is increasingly dependent on services over which he is unable to exert any influence and on experts who advise and prescribe how he is to live. His normal, inborn faculties are smothered in this welter of instructions and advice; he remains as subordinate and bereft of autonomy as a child, and is permitted—is expected— to remain so. He has no confidence in himself, in the future or in the self-regulating power of life."
>
> —Ricarda Winterswyl, *Süddeutsche Zeitung*,
> Munich, April 20, 1991

On the other hand, however, we ignore these rhythms for the simplest of possible reasons: *we don't know about them.* Perhaps you are one of the pioneers who is trying to reconquer this knowledge, slowly, unhurriedly, little by little. For it is by no means too late to revive this ancient art. It is merely waiting for people who don't make excuses. Every single action counts, no matter how small. Sometimes it can count for much more than grand gestures and grand words.

All the rules and laws presented in this book have their roots exclusively in personal experience. There is nothing that derives from hearsay, nothing based on assumptions or convictions. There are certainly many other rhythms and influencing factors in nature such as those relating to human biorhythms, to sunspot activity, to cosmic and earth radiations, and so on. However, this book restricts itself exclusively to the seven different states of the moon:

	New Moon
	Waxing Moon
	Full Moon
	Waning Moon
	Position of the moon in a sign of the zodiac
	Ascending Moon
	Descending Moon

Whether the moon and the constellation it occupies in the heavens exercise a direct influence, or whether as previously suggested the current positions of the moon and stars merely function like the hands of a clock, is a question that has yet to be answered conclusively.

The forces and their effects on humans, animals, and plants—completely irrespective of what causes them—can be proven anytime through *experience*. Research into causes will have to content itself with speculation, opinion, and conviction for the time being—but certainly not for much longer. However, for a long time now a terminology has gained acceptance, such as: "The sign Capricorn has an effect on the knee" or "The full moon influences the psyche." For the sake of simplicity we have adhered to such forms of expression in this book.

THE NEW MOON

DURING ITS APPROXIMATELY 28-day rotation around the earth, the moon always turns only one side toward this planet, the side that we can see in all its glory during the full moon. Astronomers call such a rigid revolution of a satellite about another heavenly body "fixed rotation."

If the moon lies (as seen from the earth) between the earth and the sun, then the side turned toward us is completely in darkness. It cannot then be made out, and on the earth **New Moon** prevails (also known in olden times as the "dead moon").

It is important to note that at the new moon the moon stands in front of the same backdrop of stars and hence in the same zodiac sign as the sun. This is easily understood when one considers that the moon at this time is at its nearest to the sun and thus the sun, moon, and an observer on earth almost form a single line. And so for instance in March the new moon is always in the sign of Pisces, in August it is always in Leo, and so on.

It is useful to bear this rule in mind when trying to work out roughly which zodiac sign the moon is currently in. Remember that the moon always stays for two or three days in a particular sign. So by the next full moon after the new moon in March, the moon has covered exactly half the zodiac and is thus six signs further on; according to this, fourteen days later the moon will have to be in the sign of Virgo or Libra. This principle can be applied to every other month in the year.

In calendars the new moon is usually depicted as a black disc. A short period prevails of special impulses affecting humans, animals, and plants. Anyone, for example, who fasts for a day during this period will be able to prevent many illnesses because the detoxifying power of the body is at its peak. If someone wishes to throw bad habits overboard, then this day is more suitable as a starting point than almost any other. Diseased trees will be able to recover after being cut back on this day. The earth begins to breathe in.

The impulses of the new moon days are not so strongly and directly perceptible as those of the full moon, because the switchover and reorientation of the forces from waning to waxing moon is not so violent as is the case in the reverse situation at full moon.

THE WAXING MOON

JUST A FEW hours after the new moon the side of the moon facing the earth begins to come into view—slowly moving from right to left, a graceful sickle appears. In its turn the **waxing moon**, with its own specific influences, is getting under way. The journey of about six days to the half-moon is also known as the first quarter of the moon; the period from there until the full moon, which occurs about thirteen days later, is called the second quarter.

Everything that is to be supplied to the body—that builds it up and strengthens it—works twice as well for a period of two weeks. The more the moon waxes, the more unfavorable are the prospects for healing wounds and operations. For example, even with the same amount of detergent, the laundry does not become so clean as it does when the moon is on the wane. More children come into the world when the moon is waxing and when it is full.

THE FULL MOON

Finally the moon has covered half of its journey round the earth; the side facing us appears as the **full moon**, a bright circular disc in the night sky. Seen from the viewpoint of the sun, the moon is now behind the earth. On calendars the full moon is depicted as a white disc.

In the few hours of the full moon a clearly perceptible force likewise makes itself felt on earth among humans, animals, and plants. However, the change in direction of the moon impulses from waxing to waning is felt more strongly than the changeover at new moon. "Moon-struck" people walk in their sleep, wounds bleed more profusely than at other times; medicinal herbs gathered on this day develop greater powers; trees cut back at this time could die; police stations increase their manpower because they regularly face a rise in violent crime and accidents. Midwives are called in for an emergency shift.

THE WANING MOON

Slowly the moon wanders onwards; the shadow "dents" it from right to left, as it were; the roughly 13-day phase of the waning moon begins (third and fourth quarter).

Once again our forebears deserve the credit for the discovery of special influences during this period: operations are more successful than at other times; almost all work about the house goes more smoothly; even someone who eats too much at this time will not put on weight so quickly. Many jobs in the garden and out of doors are either favored at this time (such as sowing and planting root vegetables), or else they turn out rather unfavorably (for instance grafting fruit trees).

THE MOON IN THE ZODIAC

WHEN THE EARTH travels round the sun, the latter, seen from the viewpoint of the earth, stays for a month in each of the constellations of the zodiac. The moon passes through the same zodiac signs in its 28-day orbit of the earth, though in its case it only stays about two and a half days in each sign.

The 12 different forces that are associated with the position of the moon in the zodiac can only seldom be perceived as directly as the force felt at full moon. However, the influence on plants, animals, and humans is clearly recognizable, particularly the effects on the body and health, or in the garden and on the farm (crop yields, weed control, fertilizing). For example, the moon in Virgo (whose element is earth) is regarded in the plant kingdom as a "root day." Measures taken to enhance root growth during these two or three days are more effective and successful than on other days.

Particularly in the field of medicine, the knowledge of the connection between the position of the moon and the course of illnesses used to be conscientiously observed. Hippocrates, the mentor of all physicians, knew about the lunar forces and instructed his pupils unequivocally: "Anyone who practices medicine without taking into consideration the movement of the stars is a fool." And again: "Do not operate on parts of the body that are governed by the sign through which the moon is passing."

In human beings the current position of the moon in the zodiac exercises specific influences on regions of the body and its organs. One commonly speaks of each bodily zone being "governed" by a particular sign of the zodiac. You will be able to gather the exact connections from the table summary at the end of this chapter.

Those of our ancestors skilled in the art of medicine discovered the following principles:

☾

Everything that is done for the well-being of that part of the body governed by the sign through which the moon is currently passing is more effective than on other days—with the exception of surgical operations.

Everything that puts a special burden or strain on that part of the body governed by the sign through which the moon is currently moving is more harmful than on other days.

Surgical operations on the organ or body part in question should be avoided during these days if at all possible. Emergency operations are subject to a higher law.

If the moon is waxing as it passes through the sign, then all measures taken to supply nutrient materials and strengthen the region of the body governed by the sign are more effective than when the moon is on the wane. If it is waning, then all measures taken to detoxify and relieve the organ in question are more successful than when the moon is waxing.

☾

Surgical operations are only apparently an exception to this rule. Admittedly they ultimately serve the well-being of the organ in question; however, at the moment of the operation and in the period that follows immediately after, their effect is to put a strain on the organ. These relationships will be discussed again in detail in Chapter 2.

THE ASCENDING AND DESCENDING MOON

FREQUENTLY IN THIS book we shall be referring to the **ascending** and **descending** forces of the moon. The important thing to realize is that whether the moon is ascending or descending has nothing to do with the phases of the moon, i.e., whether it is currently waning or waxing. The ascending and descending moon is a concept connected with the position of the moon in the zodiac.

All signs of the zodiac through which the sun passes in the course of a year between the winter solstice (December 21st) and the summer solstice (June 21st), consisting of Sagittarius to Gemini, possess an **ascending** force. This is the force of winter and spring, which signals gradual increase, expansion, growth, and flowering.

On the other hand a **descending** force belongs to the signs in the second half of the year, *Gemini to Sagittarius*. These are the forces of summer and autumn, which signals ripeness, harvest, decline, and rest.

The signs Gemini and Sagittarius are not generally established so exactly in this usage because they represent *turning points* between the ascending and descending forces, and for this reason it is not possible to ascribe them definitely to one or the other of the two forces. The exact distinction only becomes important in light of the particular activity one has in mind.

Now both these qualities, ascending and descending, also make themselves felt during the 28-day journey of the moon through the zodiac—almost as if the forces of spring, summer, autumn, and winter were also perceptible in the course of a single month. They contribute to the individual "color" of a given sign and exercise an effect—depending on the phase of the moon—particularly in the garden and in nature, but also in medicine.

The period of the ascending moon was also called harvest-time and the signs with descending force were known as planting time, because in farming and gardening it is extremely useful to observe these two different impulses. When the moon is ascending (from Sagittarius to Gemini), the sap is rising. Fruit and vegetables are especially juicy, and the development of plants above ground is particularly favored. When the moon is descending (from Gemini to Sagittarius), the sap is drawn more downwards and this enhances root formation.

People devised a mnemonic in order to be able to distinguish between the two impulses. When the sign ⌣ is shown in a calendar this moon sign seems like a bowl: ascending moon, the bowl is being filled up—harvest time. Conversely the sign ⌒ indicates the descending moon—planting time.

Another simple method for remembering which sign has an ascending and which a descending force requires a knowledge of the parts of the body governed by the various signs. Refer to the table at the end of the chapter.

The *Aries* and *Taurus* influence is ascending. These first two signs of the zodiac govern the upper extremities of the body, from the head to the neck and shoulder girdle. The last four signs—Sagittarius (turning point), Capricorn, Aquarius, and Pisces—are likewise ascending and govern the lower extremities: thigh, knee, lower leg, and foot. Thus all these signs of the zodiac are directed outward and run upward and sideways from the shoulder and downward from the thigh. This equals ascending force.

The "middle" six zodiac signs (Gemini to Sagittarius) are directed inward into the body and principally concern its inner organs: chest, lungs, liver, and kidneys down to the hips. This equals descending force.

COMBINED EFFECTS

THE SEVEN IMPULSES described above are able to penetrate, amplify, or deaden each another and to contribute to the reorientation of the prevailing impulse qualities.

For example, measures taken to detoxify the body when the moon is on the wane are more effective in a zodiac sign that has descending force than in a sign with ascending force. (Don't forget that all internal organs, including those that detoxify, are governed by signs with descending force.)

If for instance the moon is in Leo, which would have an unfavorable effect on a heart operation, this negative effect will be amplified many times if the moon is also waxing at the time (as is the case from February to August). On the other hand, a remedy to strengthen the heart administered in a sign *with ascending force when the moon is waxing* is more effective than the same remedy applied *when the moon is on the wane in a sign with descending force.*

We leave it to the pioneers among our readers, in particular the physicians and practitioners, to study the following rhythms and draw the appropriate conclusions.

Today many doctors and practitioners again have built up experience with these rhythms. Even protracted illnesses could often potentially be relieved using this method and with a slight shift of attitude. Observation and patience is called for here.

THE OCCURRENCE OF THE ZODIAC SIGNS IN THE VARIOUS PHASES OF THE MOON

Zodiac Sign	in Waxing Moon	in Waning Moon
Aries	October to April	April to October
Taurus	November to May	May to November
Gemini	December to June	June to December
Cancer	January to July	July to January
Leo	February to August	August to February
Virgo	March to September	September to March
Libra	April to October	October to April
Scorpio	May to November	November to May
Sagittarius	June to December	December to June
Capricorn	July to January	January to July
Aquarius	August to February	February to August
Pisces	September to March	March to September

If you do not wish to be forever looking up this table, you can make a note of the following rule of thumb:

The sign of the zodiac in which the **sun** is presently situated will from this month onwards be in the waning moon for the next six months and for six months after that will be in the waxing moon. Thus if we use March as an example, the sun is in Pisces and the new moon is in Pisces.

The following observation is especially interesting. If one combines the knowledge of the bodily regions that are governed by various zodiac signs with the information given above concerning the occurrence throughout the year of the signs of the zodiac in the different phases of the moon, and the laws attendant on this, then it follows logically that measures taken to heal certain organs and regions of the body *will have different effects in each half of the year.* This conclusion has been substantiated by experience on numerous occasions.

To take an example: hip operations (the region of the hips is governed by the sign Libra) will produce much better results in the months from October to April, when Libra is always in the waning moon, than in the other half of the year. This is provided that the operation does not take place precisely in the Libra days.

When one has grasped this principle, it is very easy to transfer it to other regions and organs of the body.

So every sign of the zodiac, each offset from its predecessor by a month, has at its disposal the sustaining power to flush out poisons for half the year, and to supply constructive materials for the other half. I discovered this connection because I always note down the time when a measure is particularly helpful or simply has a good effect. I also make a note whenever an otherwise "good" remedy, administered in favorable phases of the moon or in the appropriate sign of the zodiac, fails to produce the usual effect. From observations over many years I have come to the conclusion that certain applications in autumn, say, lead more rapidly to the desired result than in spring, and vice versa.

However, one of the most important rules is this: **carry out surgical operations whenever possible when the moon is on the wane**, even if this knowledge is hardly ever applied and is still largely unknown to doctors. It simply won't fit smoothly enough into a scientific pigeonhole. And yet even the knowledge that one should wash one's hands before operations took many years to be accepted as correct and necessary.

SPECIAL RHYTHMS

IN THIS BOOK you will also make the acquaintance of some very special rhythms: rules and dates that are completely independent of the position of the moon. They number among the most remarkable and inexplicable things between heaven and earth and we shall not even attempt to give reasons for them. How is one to explain the fact that wood cut down after sunset on March 1st will not burn provided that the logs and planks are not being dried artificially? We are confident that there are interested and curious readers who will simply try these extraordinary laws out for themselves: they are just as valid as any other rule.

THE MOMENT OF CONTACT

THERE IS ONE question that interests many people. How can it be that a particular "favorable" moment to gather fruit, say, or to take a medicine often produces very positive long-term results, whereas only a short time afterwards the opposite negative influence prevails which condemns the same action to failure? Is it not then possible for the subsequent negative energy to cancel out the positive? Potatoes, for example, last for months if they are picked and stored at the correct moment. If they are harvested only a few days earlier or later they can sometimes spoil in a very short time.

Perhaps the answer will sound a little mysterious, but it corresponds to the facts. The moment of "touching" is the decisive factor, the moment of action, whether it be on a human being, an animal, or a plant.

If I touch a living being at a particular moment—whether with my thoughts or my hands, through my inner or my outer intentions—then at that moment I transmit fine energies and in particular the forces that are characterized by the phase and zodiac sign of the moon like a magnifying glass that bundles the ambient scattered energies together and produces a greater effect with them than if they were separate.

These forces have such a powerful effect that even touching potatoes, for example, *that have already been stored* will have a different outcome depending on the moment of contact. If one realizes that potatoes are spoiling prematurely because they were picked and stored at the "wrong" moment, then it is still possible to save the situation to a considerable extent by storing them again on a *favorable* day. Conversely one can sometimes discover that stored potatoes suddenly spoil very quickly if they are touched and moved at an unfavorable moment—perhaps through sliding down after a few potatoes have been fetched for kitchen supplies.

Many apparently contradictory experiences in everyday life—in medicine, in the garden and countryside, and in the household—may perhaps find a plausible explanation here. The principle of contact may be applied to all the rules that are presented in this book.

THE LUNAR CALENDAR

YOU WILL PERHAPS have already noticed that the only technical aid required for the knowledge of natural and lunar rhythms is a *lunar calendar*—a calendar that gives the *phases of the moon* and the *position of the moon in the zodiac.* You will find just such a calendar included at the back of the book.

From countless letters from all over the world (up to now our books have been translated into 22 languages) we have discovered what is of particular interest to our readers in connection with these calendars and what experience they have had with them over the years. We are now able to pass this experience on to you.

> Our lunar calendar is calculated according to the *position of the moon in the zodiac.* All the useful experience that we pass on in our books—in the domains of medicine and medicinal herbs and ecologically sound building, in gardening, agriculture, and forestry—all of this is based on *this* calendar. We have frequently received queries because some regional lunar calendars exhibit slight differences from ours. You need not worry about this. Most of these differences arise because many lunar calendars have been calculated by astrologers or astronomers according to their own principles. If you have any doubt about the validity of a particular calendar, simply experiment with both calendars until you can be certain.
>
> The times of the new and full moon have been left out, since these alter from one time zone to another. For some activities, however, it is important to know the exact times of the phases of the moon and these can be found in most conventional calendars.

⮞ Anyone who studies astronomy and is able to identify the individual constellations of the zodiac in the night sky will discover that the "actual" position of the sun and moon differs from that given in the calendar. However, you can place your trust in the calendar. Certain deviations in the course of sun, moon, and stars over a 28,000-year cycle are responsible for this.

For this reason valid lunar calendars for thousands of years have not been calculated according to the actual position of the sun, but from the vernal equinox—when day and night are the same length—on about March 21st. The basis of these calculations is very complex; this is not the place to decipher the precise relationships. We therefore refer you to the abundant astronomical literature on the subject.

The discrepancy between the actual position of the moon and the position given in the calendar may give an indication concerning the causal relationship of the lunar rhythms; for it should be clear that the stellar constellation itself, thousands of millions of light years away, has nothing to do with our recognizing and exploiting the 12 impulses. It is not that the stars exert a force, but instead that a force exists that may be calculated with the aid of the stars.

Perhaps we might offer a suggestion: a researcher wishing to fathom the reciprocal relationship between the position of the moon and the quality of the impulse should look out for resonance phenomena arising from the revolutions and oscillations around the sun of the moon, earth, and planets—as if he were studying a multidimensional musical instrument that produced 12 clearly distinguishable tones.

Just how important resonance is, the sympathetic vibration of a body with the vibration emanating from another body, is something I discovered as a

very small child. While I was playing in the garden near a zinc bathtub I sud-
denly heard for about a minute some soft music and then the voice of some-
one reading the news. The sounds were coming from the bathtub and they
stopped the moment that I grasped hold of it. Under certain conditions the tub
had the same frequency as a radio transmitter in the vicinity, and the way it
was constructed amplified the waves and made them audible.

It is possible to calculate to the minute the shift from one zodiac sign to the next; but calendar-makers today as in all previous
ages only give the position of the moon in the zodiac for *whole*
days, and for good reasons pay no attention to over-exact methods
of measurement. The influences indicated by the position of the
moon in the zodiac overlap and merge, particularly when the calendar shows a sign three days in a row. Then the force of the neigh-
boring sign can still be felt on the first or can already be felt on the
third day. God does not work in such a petty way as compelling us
to cut our hair (successfully) only before eleven in the morning,
while after that causing hair that has been trimmed to fall out. He
has ordered nature in such a way that, for every suitable time that
is missed or spoiled by the weather, sufficient alternatives are available in order to achieve results that are nearly as good. When we
are talking about an operation for which the patient is able to spec-
ify the date, then he or she should simply look out for the waning
moon and steer well clear of the zodiac sign that governs the particular part of the body in question.

There are numerous signals in nature that indicate the change
from one sign to another, once one has begun to pay attention to
them: the penetrating light on air days (Gemini, Libra, Aquarius),
the active circulation during Leo, the differences in the way windows steam up on water days and air days, the slight headache
when Aries arrives, the digestibility of a fatty meal during Gemini,
Libra, and Aquarius, and much more. People with "intuitive" gifts

or "green thumbs" are often unconsciously guided by all these signals, which show us the most sensible way to proceed.

Nature does not allow itself to be forced into a rigid system and governed according to a set of handy formulae, even if that is what our laziness constantly cries out for. We consider that to be one of its most beautiful and life-giving qualities. The lunar calendar is a valuable aid, no less, but no more either. It is not intended as a substitute for your personal awareness and experience. On the contrary: it can serve as a key to the enlargement of your awareness.

❧ And finally, a note for readers in the Southern Hemisphere: All the rules concerning lunar and natural rhythms have the same validity for you—from South America to South Africa to Australia to New Zealand.

Slight exceptions are principally connected with the fact that the seasons are reversed where you are. Our winter is high summer for you, and when in your temperate latitudes the leaves are falling, we are being wafted by spring breezes. This difference is of especial importance in gardening, agriculture, and forestry, for instance when deciding the right time for felling timber. This should be done mainly when the sap is at rest—in temperate or cold regions between June 21 and July 6, or in tropical regions during the period of greatest heat and aridity. With a little experimentation all the guidelines in the book can effortlessly be transposed to the Southern Hemisphere with its reversed sequence of seasons.

However, perhaps the most relevant difference for you is the external form of the waxing and waning moon in the sky. In the northern hemisphere the moon waxes from right to left, in the Southern Hemisphere from left to right. Since probably 90 percent of our readers live in the Northern Hemisphere, we have depicted the symbols for the waxing and waning moon as they are to be observed in the Northern Hemisphere—the exact reverse of what you see. To make matters simpler, look at it this way: when we talk about the "waning" moon we mean the period between full moon and new moon—regardless of the form manifested in the sky or depicted in the calendar. When we talk about the "waxing" moon we mean the period between new moon and full moon—regardless of its form in the sky or in the calendar.

Ultimately it comes down to your own common sense: Take the information in this book first and foremost as a stimulus for the journey into the realm of natural and lunar rhythms. Build up your own experience, experiment, try things out. You will soon discover for yourself exactly what difference the "topsy-turvy" seasons make down under. In the long run it is definitely more profitable to gain your own experience than to have every single step prescribed for you in a book.

THE ZODIACAL TABLE

THE TABLE THAT follows is an important tool. It gives an overview of the various effects of each individual sign of the zodiac—on regions of the body, parts of plants, food qualities, and so forth—and shows the most commonly used signs of the zodiac in order to facilitate reading off the symbols in the calendars at the back of the book. You may wish to make a copy of it to consult while reading through the book.

Zodiac Sign	Symbol	Body Zone	Organ System	Plant Part	Element	Ascending/Descending	Food Quality	Day Quality
Aries		head, brain, eyes, nose	sense organs	fruit	fire	☽	protein	warm
Taurus		larynx, speech organs, teeth, jaws, throat, tonsils, ears	blood circulation	root	earth	☽	salt	cool
Gemini		shoulders, arms, hands, lungs	glandular system	flower	air	☾	fat	air/light
Cancer		chest, lungs, stomach, liver, gallbladder	nervous system	leaf	water	☾	carbohydrate	wetness
Leo		heart, back, diaphragm, circulation, artery	sense organs	fruit	fire	☾	protein	warm
Virgo		digestive organs, nerves, spleen, pancreas	blood circulation	root	earth	☾	salt	cool
Libra		hips, kidneys, bladder	glandular system	flower	air	☾	fat	air/light
Scorpio		sex organs, ureter	nervous system	leaf	water	☾	carbohydrate	wetness
Sagittarius		thigh, veins	sense organs	fruit	fire	☽	protein	warm
Capricorn		knee, bones, joints, skin	blood circulation	root	earth	☽	salt	cool
Aquarius		lower leg, veins	glandular system	flower	air	☽	fat	air/light
Pisces		feet, toes	nervous system	leaf	water	☽	carbohydrate	wetness

T W O

Healthy Living in Harmony with Lunar Cycles

DO YOU THINK YOU CAN TAKE OVER THE UNIVERSE
AND IMPROVE IT?
I DO NOT BELIEVE IT CAN BE DONE.

THE UNIVERSE IS SACRED.
YOU CANNOT IMPROVE IT.
IF YOU TRY TO CHANGE IT, YOU WILL RUIN IT.
IF YOU TRY TO HOLD IT, YOU WILL LOSE IT.

SO SOMETIMES THINGS ARE AHEAD AND SOMETIMES THEY ARE BEHIND;
SOMETIMES BREATHING IS HARD, SOMETIMES IT COMES EASILY;
SOMETIMES THERE IS STRENGTH AND SOMETIMES WEAKNESS,
SOMETIMES ONE IS UP AND SOMETIMES DOWN.

THEREFORE THE SAGE AVOIDS EXTREMES, EXCESSES AND COMPLACENCY.

—Lao Tsu

REFLECTIONS ON HEALTH

EVERYONE THINKS HE knows what health means. And yet only a few years ago it was officially defined at the highest level by the World Health Organization as the "absence of illness"—perhaps precisely because it is only when it is lacking that one feels health to be the "highest good." In spite of this nothing could be further from the truth; and many doctors and practitioners today are making an effort to see things from a new perspective. Thus a renowned German physician and author writes: "For us health means the power and capacity to become what we are and to overcome whatever stands in our way; it describes the state that results from this: a harmonious interplay of the various processes that define a human being in the service of an intention that pursues the meaning of life."

Our ancestors knew about these ideas. Priest-physicians, shamans, and medicine men, skilled in the art of healing, acted on the knowledge that we humans are not machines; that we are more than a system of bones, nerves, muscles, and organs held together by evolutionary chance; that body, mind, and soul mutually influence each other and form an inseparable unity with everything around us—with other human beings, with nature, even with the stars.

They knew that illness arises whenever a human being, for whatever reason, can no longer maintain the dynamic, flowing equilibrium between the many elements of life—between tension and relaxation, between healthy egoism and devotion, between the ups and downs of fate.

Everything in nature is sound, vibration, and rhythm. A balanced life thus means that one does not *continually* disregard the cyclic rhythms to which our body is subject or constantly try to swim against the stream. On the other hand, balance has nothing to do with the rhythm of the clock, with laziness and a sluggish, lukewarm ebbing away of time. Measured doses of excess are just as important for healthy living as regularity and rhythm in daily life. Every organ, every living creature from time to time requires its share of stimuli—shocks, so to speak—in order to push forward to the limits of its developmental potential.

Our body is like a robust and dependable ship, which requires a certain degree of maintenance in order to deliver its full performance, or the performance corresponding to its age, and which needs a more or less regular supply of fuel in the form of oxygen and a variety of foodstuffs. And it is not only the body that needs food but also the mind and the soul. The peculiar scientific picture of the world that dominates the modern mind has almost caused us to forget that in the vessel that is the body, our feelings, thoughts and instincts also have an important part to play, and that, most important of all, it is waiting for a captain: consciousness.

It is our consciousness, our attitude toward life, which helps to determine the fate of our body and exerts an influence on bodily health, efficiency, and the enjoyment of life. At the same time it affects the fate of the natural environment. The state of the latter is always an exact reflection of our own state, physically as well as mentally.

What is meant by "attitude"? Imagine that you are wearing your best clothes on a Sunday outing. To the malicious pleasure of bystanders, a glob of bird-droppings lands with a juicy splash on your shoulder. Now what? Rage will bring you a step nearer to a stomach ulcer or a heart attack; self-pity will strengthen your feeling of your own importance and could do you even more damage. But you could just as well go home whistling happily to yourself and clean the special garment, with a heartfelt expression of thanks to God on your lips for not having endowed cows with wings . . .

Seriously: there are of course far worse things in life than dirty jackets. However, a good captain knows that his *attitude* influences and determines a great many things. He or she knows that the "disease of the foregone conclusion" is far worse than any other and is at pains not to take anything for granted, in good fortune and in bad. Disappointments in life are always just as great as the hopes and expectations that one cherished beforehand. And the captain also knows that simply being master of a fast ship does not make him or her a better navigator, let alone someone with a good sense of direction.

Our body is truly a marvelous thing. For years on end it apparently forgives everything: faulty nourishment, lack of exercise, excess of alcohol and nicotine, stress, and long-standing disregard for its natural rhythms. That is also what makes a change in living habits so difficult: so much has become cherished routine that one no longer has the desire to give it up. And we know so little about the true requirements and rhythms of our body.

In order to become an experienced and benevolent "manager" of your own life you have to know how your body functions, what the tolerable limits of pollution are, and under what conditions it will deliver its maximum efficiency. Great courage is needed for this: the courage to recognize that one sometimes reaps what one has sown, in terms of neglecting our own needs, and that our whole life is subject to cycles—with peaks *and* troughs, highs *and* lows.

In the West we are living through a reign of "fitness terror." We are pressured to be always fit, always beautiful, always in top form, always ready. This ideal is almost a declaration of war on nature, for she also imposes on us troughs in the waves, and we would do well to get to accept them. It takes courage nowadays to be able to face downward movements with a cool head and calm awareness—to be able to accept them without resisting, deadening one's feelings, or getting upset. It really does exist: plain common sense. Anyone who has learned to listen to it knows that: "There are no hills without valleys."

MAN CANNOT HAVE GOOD TIMES FOR A THOUSAND DAYS,

ANY MORE THAN A FLOWER CAN BLOOM FOR A HUNDRED DAYS.

—*Tseng-Kuang*

It is a fundamental duty to look after our body and our environment. "Civilization" deadens the feeling for this duty, among other reasons because in so many spheres of life we are able to surrender responsibility for ourselves ("It doesn't matter: after all, I am insured . . .").

If we manage to show even a single reader just how easy and enjoyable it is to submit to the rhythms of nature, out of friendship toward oneself, then we shall have achieved a great deal. Only someone who is his own best friend can be a friend to his fellow men. The old and proven knowledge of natural cycles deserves to be gratefully tested before one makes up one's mind that "there's no such thing."

Where previously a calm weighing up of possibilities and alternatives determined one's way of life, nowadays the principle of comfort holds sway—comfort and apparently limitless possibilities. Whether it is our health that is in danger, or the health of nature: the law of reason, not comfort, should come first. We do not need to, nor ought we, renounce progress and technology. But our watchword should be "moderation in all things." We must not lose sight of moderation. Then a rational life and an intact environment will be possible—making full use of research and technology.

Just in the last decades medicine has made enormous progress and has been able to help many people. If it is now possible to convince these really excellent medical people that there are laws and cycles that can have a very favorable—and sometimes a very unfavorable—effect on our lives and bodies, then humanity will have made another step forward.

CAUSE AND THERAPY

THERE ARE THOUSANDS of hints and tips for a healthy lifestyle. Apart from the fact that it would be impossible to list them all, it would be downright boring. So in this chapter we should like to restrict ourselves mainly to those that are connected with the lunar cycles. One or two of the hints (as well as some of the rules in Chapter 3) have nothing to do with the path of the moon and are based on personal experience or on other rhythms.

However, no book that offers advice on health should fail to give some assistance in tracing the underlying causes of illness. At the start of every therapy the question should be posed: "Where does the illness come from?"—not the question: "How can I get rid of it as quickly as possible?" We should be able to look the cause straight in the face. Otherwise any therapy will come to a halt with a treatment of the symptoms; the cause will remain untouched and will continue to exert an influence.

A thorough answer to the question concerning the cause is already almost the whole diagnosis and half the therapy. At this point there are two possible wrong turns. One can settle for the answer: "I've got a cold, because I've been infected." Or else one can spend three days of brooding soul-searching and put the blame on one's parents and forebears. Neither approach will be any help to you.

You should give up searching for someone who could be "to blame" for an illness. It should never be a matter of identifying villains: our body, which doesn't "want" to do what we want of it, our mind, our parents, our past, the pressure of events. This often only serves to excuse our own inactivity and allows us to go on cursing fate. Furthermore, if you are one of those people who expect miracles from a medicine, or at least that it should work by itself without your active involvement, then you won't get much from this book. For it will only yield a genuine profit if you work with it— if you treat it as a challenge to train yourself to be alert.

When you have found an honest answer to the question of cause, a doctor will also be in a much better position to help you because you will be able to work together and you will no longer have the all-too common attitude of "I'm ill. Set me free from my illness." Doctors can only help you to help yourself. They can help you to awaken your own powers of self-healing. If deep down in yourself you haven't the slightest interest in getting well—because illness brings you attention, because it allows you to evade other responsibilities, because it seems like a good way out of a difficult situation, because admitting your own responsibility for the illness is too uncomfortable, and so on—then no doctor will be able to help you. And this book least of all.

Before the knowledge of lunar cycles can be of genuine value for a healthy lifestyle, a certain insight is necessary: the causes of illness are often not to be sought in our bodies, but in the breeding ground of false and destructive habits of thought, often connected with competitiveness, anxiety, and greed. These are often the real cause underlying the "many sins against nature" that Hippocrates mentions.

Anyone who casts a cool, objective glance in the mirror will not be able to reject these weaknesses immediately. It is this objective look at oneself that will enable you to make the best possible use of the tips on the following pages.

Once again it must be explicitly pointed out that this book can never replace and is never intended to replace a doctor. No one should feel that they should treat an illness single-handedly without the advice of a physician.

At my lectures people sometimes tell me about good and not-so-good doctors. I think that there are only good doctors, but there certainly are some that are less successful with some treatments. The correct timing of the start of a course of treatment is often decisive. At first of course in conversations with doctors about the moon and its influence I sensed a deep mistrust. But every one of them that took the trouble to check back in his records and compare successful and unsuccessful recoveries with the position of the moon at the time, was inevitably amazed. Now, thank goodness, there are many doctors who in their various treatments pay attention to the lunar cycle. Especially in the case of recurrent or chronic clinical pictures there is a good chance of picking out favorable moments for treatment.

GOOD DIET, GOOD DIGESTION—
THE MAIN PILLARS OF HEALTH

YOUR FOOD SHOULD BE YOUR MEDICINE.

—*Hippocrates*

EVERYONE HAS EXPERIENCED this: certain minor or major ailments can be tackled with certain medicines, ointments, and infusions. Recovery is rapid and often the symptoms disappear forever. But on another occasion the nursing and treatment is in vain, and the conviction slowly creeps up on you that nothing is going to do any good.

First of all we have to find out whether the treatment was sensible anyway and what diagnosis was given. A blood-cleansing tea will not be effective when what is indicated is an antispasmodic; pain-relieving drugs will only remove the symptom if the actual cause is to be found in overeating, too little liquid intake, and so on.

Often the diagnosis reveals that the factor triggering off an illness is an imbalance in diet and digestion. In this context good digestion in particular is of central importance for a healthy life. Numerous minor and major disorders and illnesses start off in poor diet and disturbed digestion. At the same time few subjects in health care and the treatment of illness are so neglected and beset with taboos as our digestive processes. Formerly, for the best of reasons, it was taken for granted that doctors and practitioners would immediately inquire about the composition of the patient's stool and from this would draw extremely valuable conclusions for diagnosis and therapy. The saying "You are what you eat" is not without a certain truth. Everything entering our body can become either poison or medicine, depending on the ingredients and quantities, and, as you will see, depending also to a large extent on the moment when it is ingested.

First and foremost, any kind of one-sided nutrition, any kind of "diet"—except in the case of certain illnesses—is positively harmful. This is a piece of advice that you've certainly often heard before, and maybe you're sick and tired of hearing it. But hold on a moment. One-sidedness is detrimental, no matter how "healthy" the food is. The body certainly needs more than just "health-giving grain" or "roughage." Please don't misunderstand us: we eat health-giving grain, too, and roughage is something that everyone needs. But a certain variety is necessary in order to keep the digestive organs on the go, just as every muscle needs movement in order to maintain full efficiency.

Another important point is that many people with problems of digestion are inclined to take *exaggerated* measures. Generally, as is so often the case, what lies at the bottom of this is impatience and the expectation of rapid results. However, patterns of behavior and eating habits that have been practiced for years cannot be altered overnight; and even if they are the body only reacts slowly to changes, just as a soil that has been spoiled reacts slowly to natural methods of cultivation. It needs time in order to remember what is natural and adapted to the rhythms of nature. Often the intestine has to learn again how to discern its own signals.

Already in school our natural digestive rhythms were trained out of us. The digestive processes have to wait until the lesson, or even the whole morning, is over. Generally we are ourselves too lazy to get up early enough for there to be time both for a leisurely breakfast and some "urgent business" in the toilet. If something is wrong with our digestion, then almost always what is needed is a minor or major change in our living and eating habits.

If for example the digestive processes get out of balance and this manifests itself in constipation, then the poisons that are normally expelled in regular bowel movements simply remain too long within the body and are partially reabsorbed by the large intestine.

One of the most effective ways to return to regular and healthy digestion is to *pay attention to the body's signals.* Almost everyone has experienced this: if we ignore the signal for a bowel movement only for a few minutes, then it sometimes takes hours or even days before the signal returns. You now know what happens in these hours. Of course it is not always easy to interrupt school lessons or business transactions with the words: "Would you excuse me for a moment . . . ?" But the alternative is self-poisoning. Irritated looks from those present just betray their attitude. Pay no attention to those sidelong glances and do your health a favor.

A dogmatic toilet hypochondriac who is meticulously attentive to "regularity" is of course equally mixed up. Every person has his own rhythm—the goal should be to get to know it and try to do it justice.

Books, radio, television, and above all magazines are brimming with advice about "healthy diet." Only the day before yesterday potatoes and spaghetti were the great fatteners; yesterday potatoes had become the number one slimming diet; today pasta has been elevated to the status of a power food. Today fat (cholesterol) has become the villain of the piece; on the other hand, a human being cannot survive without fat. And what will it say in the papers tomorrow? Without an instinct for what is sensible and in keeping with nature, we will constantly be torn this way and that from one "ideal" diet to another, from one guide to the next. In all ages there have been guidelines concerning nutrition, but people never spoke of "diet" in the current sense of the word but instead a sensible, harmonious form of nutrition, which, with the addition of various herbs, had both a preventive and a curative effect. (By "diet" here we do not mean the vital nutritional directions given for certain illnesses: these are sensible and important.)

Up to the Breast

One day a fat pig came to a river.

He looked longingly over at the other bank, for there he could see a wonderful, freshly laid out compost heap with leftovers, potato peelings and all sorts of other delicacies gleaming enticingly across at him.

But the pig could not swim. "I wonder how deep the river is," he said to himself. "Can I simply wade across?"

"Of course you can!" said a mole, who had just emerged from his molehill and had overheard what the pig was saying.

"Do you really think so?" said the pig eagerly.

"Go ahead: the water's quite shallow," replied the mole.

He had hardly uttered the last word before the pig had run down to the water's edge and jumped in. For a moment he sank beneath the surface, because his feet were groping helplessly for the bottom. With his last ounce of strength he floundered and paddled to the bank, where he took the mole furiously to task.

"That's strange," said the mole. "On the ducks the water only comes up to their breast."

Perhaps the following tips will be able to unravel a few knotty problems for you and gradually lead to an entirely personal and unmistakable instinct for what does you good and what does not.

For that is the only thing that counts—not guidelines, rules, and principles.

THE INFLUENCE OF THE POSITION OF THE MOON ON DIET

Before we come to the specific influences of lunar phase and position in the zodiac, it might be useful to give a fundamental description of two important phases of the moon in connection with a healthy lifestyle and diet:

THE WAXING MOON

supplies, plans, takes in, builds up, absorbs, breathes in, stores energy, gathers strength, and is conducive to rest and recovery.

THE WANING MOON

washes out, detoxifies, removes, sweats out and breathes out, hardens, dries, and is conducive to action and the expenditure of energy.

If you become aware of the differing effects of these two moon phases then you will already have taken a great step toward integrating the lunar cycles harmoniously into your daily life. And you don't simply have to take this on trust. Observe for yourself, watch and investigate—you will be able to perceive and recognize these influences yourself.

Whether or not a meal agrees with us is frequently also the "responsibility" of the position of the moon. When the moon is waxing, we feel full much more frequently and gain weight more easily than when the moon is on the wane even when our eating habits and food quantities are identical. Conversely, when the moon is waning one can eat more than usual without immediately putting on weight.

An important influence on diet and digestion is exerted not only by the *phase* of the moon, but also by the *position* of the moon in the zodiac. This factor is still totally ignored by nutritionists and has all but disappeared from our awareness. Admittedly a balanced diet is recommended, but there is always the underlying thought that every kind of foodstuff—protein, carbohydrate, fat, minerals, and vitamins—should appear on the plate, if possible at the same time. It doesn't have to be, in fact it ought not to be, like this.

Cast your mind back, look around you. It is not only children that have strange phases of "eating like a horse." For a few days they simply can't get enough bulging sandwiches; then at another time it's fruit and vegetables that they want. But these cravings usually only last a couple of days.

So if on some days we happen only to want salad and on others only bread (to take a somewhat extreme example), then this has absolutely nothing to do with a one-sided diet. After all, in the course of several days the body gets everything that it needs.

Any kind of one-sidedness in diet is harmful, of course. But that does not mean that a meal has to contain everything that is "healthy." One-sidedness and a "simple" meal are very different things. Years ago people knew that, and as a matter of course they used to follow a form of selective diet. Only rarely did potatoes, vegetables, assorted side salads, meat, cheese, and raw fruit and vegetables appear at the same time on the table.

In the following table you will be able to see the reason for this. It describes the interrelationship between the position of the moon in the zodiac and the "food quality" of a given day.

THE INFLUENCE OF THE POSITION OF THE MOON ON DIET

Warmth days   *Element: fire*   *Plant part: fruit*

Aries

Leo   *Food quality: protein*

Sagittarius

These days have the best **protein qualities**. This has special effects on the physical body and the sense organs.

Cool days   *Element: earth*   *Plant part: root*

Taurus

Virgo   *Food quality: salt*

Capricorn

It is here that the best **salt qualities** prevail, which are favorable for nourishing the blood.

Light days   *Element: air*   *Plant part: flower*

Gemini

Libra   *Food quality: fat*

Aquarius

These have the best **fat and oil qualities** and they supply the glandular system.

Water days   *Element: water*   *Plant part: leaf*

Cancer

Scorpio   *Food quality: carbohydrate*

Pisces

These days possess good **carbohydrate qualities** and influence the nervous system.

What is the meaning of "food quality"—say, for instance, when with the moon in Gemini, "good fat and oil qualities" prevail? This is not an easy question to answer. A broad field opens up for research and for the branch of science known as chronobiology. Olive farmers and bakers might well venture an answer of their own to this question: during the air days of Gemini, Libra, and Aquarius it is possible to extract much more oil from olives than on any other days. On the carbohydrate days of Cancer, Scorpio, and Pisces, bakers are able to observe that their shelves often empty much more quickly than usual.

The course of the moon through the signs of the zodiac can be viewed as the circling of the hand of a clock, which in stages of two to three days indicates changing impulses affecting our food and the ability of the body to utilize it. On an oil day the oil contained in an olive behaves in a special way, differently than on other days, and the capacity of our body to make optimal use of this oil likewise changes. In other words: the harmonious interplay between food plant and body is also dependent on the timing of the meal.

However, you should not expect from these striking influences any handy system, any formula or diet that you can unerringly follow from now on. Only your own personal observation will unlock for you the full extent and value of this information. Some people can digest bread particularly well on water days (Cancer, Scorpio, Pisces), while others get a bloated belly after two slices. But patience: after only a few weeks or months, using this table and armed with one of the attached calendars, you will be able to determine exactly which food is particularly good or bad for you and on which days.

    ❧ If for example your glandular system is slightly disturbed, then you should pay close attention to what foods are particularly tasty for you on **air days** (Gemini, Aquarius, Libra). Then you will discover that precisely the "wrong" things taste especially good, and that a slight correction is required in your menu. It is definitely easier to go without certain foods a few days in the month than to keep all one's life to a strict dietary regime. This is how you can proceed on other days, too.

☙ If, for instance, you are especially fond of eating bread or other flour-based foods on **water days** (Cancer, Scorpio, Pisces) and have problems with your weight, then you should try eating easily digestible types of bread on these days, and should steer clear of meals with a high carbohydrate content (farinaceous foods).

☙ **Earth days** (Taurus, Virgo, Capricorn) have an especially strong influence on the salt quality. On these days it would be better to avoid large quantities of bacon, ham, salted herrings, fatty cheese, and the like. If your doctor has prescribed food that is low in salt then these days are particularly tricky. Many people absorb salt in especially large quantities precisely on these days, so they have to be doubly careful at this time. Unfortunately on just these "harmful" days they often have a special craving for salt. By following the motto "just this once" the good effects of a whole month of abstinence from salt can be completely ruined. But observation will gradually show the way and make you better prepared for these days.

☙ On **warmth days** (Aries, Leo, Sagittarius) you should observe whether your menu contains a noticeably large or small quantity of protein or fruit, and what affect this has on you. Warmth days are also fruit days, because the fruit part of the plant is especially favored at this time.

Of course it is difficult to make observations and draw conclusions when your meals have already been planned in advance, or if you have pre-made food waiting for you. But even then it is possible to establish whether something tasted good, or whether a meal sits heavy on your stomach and leaves behind an unpleasant feeling of heaviness as a side effect—valuable insights for when you are able to decide on your menu for yourself. Remember here our basic rule: If you feel tired after a meal, then always and without exception you have ingested something that disagrees with you and will be to your detriment in the long run. Of course tiredness after a meal is so commonplace today that you can even find doctors telling you that this is "normal." Nothing can be farther from the truth. The whole story about this fact can be found in our book *Everything's Allowed.* Therefore any change in a positive direction, however small, counts for something.

It is also valuable to notice varying reactions to the same food. Does it happen that something fatty is good for you one day, but not a week later, and then later it tastes really good again? Take a look at the moon calendar and make a short note; then in the course of time draw your own conclusions.

If the rhythm gets going in such a way that on fruit days (Aries, Leo, Sagittarius) you only feel like eating protein foods or fruit, or if on root days (Taurus, Virgo, Capricorn) you help yourself to salty food, then this isn't a bad rhythm, as long as it does you good. There is no need to labor the point that "doing good" and "tasting good" are often two different things. Such attentive observation can become especially important for people who are *allergic* so long as the allergy is not life-threatening: food that triggers off an allergy may not be equally harmful on all days. With the aid of a moon calendar one can easily find out what sort of an influence a particular day has on the allergen.

In general one can say this: if you take into account the four food qualities in the course of the month, giving the current quality greater emphasis and building it one-sidedly into your diet, then you can't go far wrong. At the very least you will rapidly establish whether you are one of those for whom this rhythm applies; for many people, however, the currently prevailing quality is precisely the one they cannot take, and thus on the contrary they have to reduce the type of food in question. Here, too, it would be advantageous to help the body's signals to make themselves felt and deliberately to put certain dishes on the table (e.g. in the case of high blood pressure, less salt on root days; and with a high cholesterol level, less fat on flower days).

Here is an example: During colds hunger is mostly absent, and rightly so. Don't eat anything, or at least not anything heavy and not in the amounts you normally eat. Every animal if it is ill or wounded instinctively knows what to do: it stops eating and rests. Each digestive process uses up some energy first before the body places the energy once more at our disposal.

Observe, watch, be aware—and take notes. Experience is what counts, not this book on its own. It is only intended to serve as an aid for you.

GENERAL ADVICE FOR A HEALTHY DIET

From my own experience I know many more rules for a healthy diet, some of which have nothing directly to do with the position of the moon. I don't want to keep them from you, because they shouldn't be left out of a discussion of this subject, and as far as I am aware they are still largely unknown.

❧ Fasting—a shorter or longer period without solid food— has become fashionable in recent years. Basically there is nothing much to be said against this, particularly when it is intended as a health cure to give the body an opportunity to detoxify and regenerate itself. As a means to losing weight it is almost never successful in the long run. Very seldom can detrimental eating habits be gotten rid of by force. The rules to follow in order successfully to give up bad habits will be discussed later in the book.

However, fasting in the sense of a marked reduction in the quantity of food consumed also often has an extremely positive effect. Not without reason, Carnival is followed by Lent, a fasting period determined by the moon. It is very good to exercise moderation in one's eating during this period, because the body detoxifies and regenerates itself particularly well at this time. It will reward such a measure with increased powers of resistance and greater well-being.

Less well known is the Advent fast (The first Sunday in Advent until December 24th), which is likewise a very favorable time to live a little more abstemiously. Nowadays of course this is difficult to achieve, but perhaps this information can nonetheless be of use to you. One thing is certain at all events: cakes and pastries eaten before Christmas are much more fattening than the goodies we munch during the Christmas period itself.

A fasting day at new moon prevents a number of illnesses. On this day the body detoxifies itself especially effectively. The ingestion of food can slow down this process or stop it altogether.

In general it is also advantageous to eat less in the days *before full moon* and *at full moon itself.* In any case many people unconsciously eat more when the moon is waning than when it is waxing, and this does not make them any fatter.

⮿ There is one very important rule relating to the *combination of foods*. You should always see to it that foods growing above ground and below ground are in well-balanced proportion in your diet. Any imbalance will have consequences that affect the entire person, physically *and* mentally. This effect is not easy to describe. One cannot positively say that it makes someone more lethargic or ponderous: that would be too crude a simplification. Neither can the difference in character between nations be simply put down to different eating habits. And yet in both assertions there is a grain of truth that cannot be ignored. Make your own observations; then you will be able to delve further into this subject and draw your own conclusions. For example, you can observe the physique and general agility of athletes from countries where people eat a great deal of the underground parts of plants and compare them with athletes from other countries in which vegetables and fruit growing above ground are a specialty.

It is always a good idea to sprinkle parsley, chives, or other herbs over potatoes. They may not balance the latter in terms of quantity, but they have powers within them that can counteract the "subterranean" emphasis.

In general it is true to say that it is not easy for everyone to digest two varieties of vegetable at the same time. One should not eat all the various sorts of food together, but one after the other. Vegetables that do not form a harmonious plant community in the garden do not belong together on the plate either, if one has a sensitive stomach. Take a look at the table of favorable and unfavorable plant communities in Chapter 3. This can serve as a useful guideline for healthy combinations of vegetable dishes.

You should be warned against two common food combinations: *whole meal products and caffeine* taken at the same time are harmful for the body. The effect involves body *and* mind. Susceptibility to headaches and migraine is greater, and in the long term a certain aggressiveness and impatience can set in.

Likewise the very popular combination of *cheese and grapes* often has similar effects. In both cases many people don't notice anything at all, but for some the results are serious, all the more so because it is difficult to detect the cause, since the connection is unknown.

✦ *The sequence of dishes.* Perhaps you will be surprised by this rule, for in many cases other customs have become established among us: *raw food should always be eaten before cooked.* Fruit or nuts before lettuce and raw vegetables. Then, for example, sour cream, bread, or milk. And only then, finally, foods that are harder to digest, such as fat, meat, eggs, cheese, and last of all dessert. Your stomach will thank you if you keep to this sequence.

✦ *Spelt and green corn:* Spelt is an unassuming, hardy wheat variety that was formerly widespread throughout the whole of Europe; in recent times it has only been cultivated sporadically, but today it is gradually gaining in importance once more. When it is harvested while it is still green, and then smoked, it is known as "green corn." Spelt is sold in the form of various grades of ground flour, coarse meal, and wheat flakes, as well as ready cooked items (spelt pancakes and green spelt patties). **Take our advice: in the kitchen, whenever possible, instead of other flours use *spelt flour!***

It's a mystery why spelt experienced such a decline after people had been feeding themselves on this valuable cereal for literally thousands of years. Hildegard von Bingen (1098–1179), the great naturalist and mystic of the Middle Ages, called it "the grain for human beings."

However it is not our purpose here to make a plea for spelt. One or two pieces of information should be enough to make you curious about this natural medicine. Some of them originate from a farmer friend of ours who has done intensive work on spelt:

Spelt contains, in harmoniously balanced proportions, practically all the nutrients that humans need—and not just in the husk, but finely distributed throughout the entire grain. This means that it retains its outstanding nutritional value even when very finely ground. Infants fed exclusively on spelt flour and water showed no deficiency symptoms, in contrast to a milk diet. Spelt is suited in the highest degree as a dietary supplement for invalids.

In contrast to most cultivated cereal varieties, spelt is genetically sound; its health value and its inner strength is incomparably higher. The harvested grain can be used as seed, whereas with the usual cereal varieties this is no longer possible. Think about it: What *real* life can be contained in flour made from grain whose power to reproduce has been artificially removed? Spelt is resistant to radioactivity and environmental poisons, because the grain is tightly enclosed in several layers of husk. After the nuclear disaster at Chernobyl it was the only harvest produce that remained immune.

• *In the evenings go without fatty foods.* The circulation, liver, and gallbladder have their high and low phases during the night, as you can gather from the table of organ cycles in this chapter. Fat-rich evening meals place an additional burden on these organs and prevent them from functioning optimally.

❧ There is an old rule: *No meat on Wednesdays and Fridays.* It has lost none of its validity.

❧ Cooking pots nowadays are made of a variety of materials: steel, iron, Teflon, copper, and others. Our recommendation is to use *enameled cooking pots*: this is still the best material. Make a comparison: prepare a meal in a steel or copper pot and next to it prepare the same quantities and ingredients in an enamel pot; then taste and smell the difference. Of course nobody expects you to throw away your old pots. If you want or have to go on using steel ones, for instance, then at least take care from now on *not to heat them too high.* In that way you can reduce some of the negative effects on the food.

Dieticians should make a study of the composition of food that has been cooked in pots made of different materials. The results would certainly confirm what has been stated here.

❧ Provisions shouldn't be bought simply according to an arbitrary weekly plan, but also a little according to the mood and need of the moment. A meal plan drawn up using the zodiac calendar will make this task a pleasure.

℃

THE TRUTH IN THE PRICE
℄

FOR MANY PEOPLE, simply the wish to cook, eat, and take care of one's body in a healthy and humanitarian manner is sufficient enough to opt for organic products. Many people waver though when every cent counts and they have to decide between cheap industrial tomatoes and somewhat more expensive organically grown tomatoes. Sometimes, despite all the insight, the decision between that which is ostensibly cheap/lifeless and that which is somewhat expensive/organic/alive is not easy.

Choose from organically cultivated crops and naturally raised livestock, for in the long run it costs only a fraction of what you have to pay for normal food, ready-to-eat meals, and industrial cosmetics. Let's spend a few moments on a new concept that has caught on only in the last few years—*true price.*

Let's assume you want to buy a pound of whole wheat grain and have the choice between "cheap" wheat produced by mega-industries or a pound of organic grain which costs a few dollars more but which doesn't cause any damage to the environment in cultivating, caring, harvesting, or processing it.

And now let's take the cheap wheat and make our way with the little package to a very special cashier. At this cashier we have added to our cheap price a few additional things that eventually bring us to the final price. Among them:

The actual energy costs of cultivating, harvesting, and distributing products. You know how environmentally damaging energy can be if coal, natural gas, petroleum oil, and atomic energy serve as their basis. Every kilowatt would have to cost hundreds of times the usual price if one were to tack on to the price the damage to the environment and public health.

The costs if the producer were to receive appropriate prices. This is never the case. "Cheap" goods are nearly always obtained through the exploitation of nature and of human labor. In most places around the world, farmers receive the least for their products and are most in need of public subsidies. Behind the retail prices of items on the shelves are an array of costs that are accrued from processing, transport, storage, packaging, advertising, and big business profits.

The costs if the producer would rely exclusively on nontoxic and environmentally compatible fertilizer and pest control methods, or as the case may be, the costs of cleaning the environment of industrial poisons—agricultural as well as foodstuff and cosmetic producers. What do environmental and health damage from this preservative or from that food taste additive cost proportionally? Only in very rare cases is the producer required to pay the damage caused by his product. And no one as yet has gone about tracing to a single foodstuff company or additive producer the sicknesses that their products indirectly help cause. That's hardly possible because they all can refer to scientists who have proven the harmlessness of their products. If the costs worldwide of destroying the environment for the sake of winning some extra grassland would be calculated into the cost of a hamburger, then it would cost hundreds of times as much.

The costs that are incurred by the large industrial producers' destruction of countless valuable and essential job positions. Almost everywhere in the Third World, small farmers are being starved out and driven to poverty in the outskirts of the big cities. These countries are thereby losing the most important pillars of self-sufficiency and independence. But that means nothing to the reigning politicians there.

The same process is taking place in the industrialized countries of the earth. Everywhere "consolidation" is practiced for the sake of short-term profit, which in the long run is at the cost of everyone else. Happily there are signs of light on the horizon and the number of organic farmers has been steadily on the increase since 1990.

We add all these costs to the purchase price of a pound of wheat. We would have to reach very deep into our pockets if we had to pay for all that together: paying more than ten times the price charged by the supermarket. That is its *true cost*. And a lot of other factors that would make the wheat even more expensive haven't even been mentioned here!

With the same amount of household money your bag of groceries might weigh a little less when buying organic foods. But isn't organic food worth it?

The true cost of real foodstuffs is very different. You can only eat half as much as usual if you switch to organic food, and would nevertheless gain more life juices and vitality from it than you would from twice that amount of produce from the food factories. The inherent energy in natural foods is in no way reflected by its price. Two naturally raised tomatoes radiate from within, giving you strength, color, and delight for hours. Two artificially ripened greenish red hothouse plastic balls carrying the "tomato" label cover your fluid needs for a half hour and cost the liver a sleepless night of attempting to get rid of its chemical residue.

Sensible experiments on animals have shown that wild animals will go for organic foods without exception when given the choice between normal (injected and chemically fertilized) or untreated vegetables.

To put it simply: If true cost were the dominant consideration in all products, then in the long run we would have no environmental problems.

If all our voluntary purchase decisions were based on information about interrelationships and true costs, then in the long run there would be no environmental problems.

"The customers don't want that," or "there's no demand" or "it's too expensive for the customers"—the responses we get at times when we ask the store managers why there are no environmentally neutral, organic products on the shelves. Really? The customers really don't want any? There's no demand?

Isn't it curious? If you poison your neighbor's child, then you'd be held responsible for it and punished. When large industries protected by politicians do the same, then nothing at all happens. This is the way the vicious circle looks:

1. Worldwide industrial combines and multinationals still earn their money today from products deleterious to health and the environment. When one country adjusts its laws, they move to another country and send us their stuff by mail.

2. Sums that would make your head spin are earned in the fight against diseases caused or unleashed by these environmental and health damaging products.

3. Obscene amounts are earned through the battle against environmental damage caused or unleashed by these products.

4. The very same industries that are making giant profits on health and environmentally damaging products are making huge amounts of money on medicines designed to fight diseases that are created by their own products.

5. Somewhere in between are the health insurance companies who throw away the money we give them fighting the symptoms of sickness but who do practically nothing in terms of health care.

6. Many of our elected servants, called "politicians," are highly dependent on these industries for election campaign contributions.

Just ask yourself now: who has a sincere interest in our health and environment? Those who earn money from sickness and harm? There's a lot of money to be earned from recycling garbage, but not from avoiding making garbage. There's lots of money to be made from combating sickness, but not from health care. Seemingly cheap prepared foods are pushed on us, but seemingly expensive organic products are not.

Recognizing this situation, this vicious cycle, is one thing, but breaking out of it is something else. If you argue with it, complain self-pityingly about it, curse at it, you will not change it, but only get bitter or despondent.

It is not so difficult to bring light into the world: if you do not accept the vicious circle, do not take part in it, then you'll succeed. For yourself and for all of us. The future of our world stands and falls with a single factor: *with your personal, individual, unbiased insight and with the power of your free will to live according to that insight.* Your free will, your purchasing decisions, your daily small decisions for or against some-thing—these are what decide the world's fate, irrespective of what political party you're inclined toward or what creed you may cherish. Untiringly we will work now and in the future to make you conscious of this great personal power and potential influence on our collective future.

If you decide on a pound of locally produced, organically grown tomatoes instead of buying sprayed and pampered life-less hothouse tomatoes, you've brought the whole world nearer to a more attractive future for us all. It's a decision of greater consequence than any political speech. You're of the opinion that a single person can't make a difference anyway? That conviction is a nightmare that colors your whole life gray on gray and is in part responsible for almost every one of your problems.

You cannot tear off a single rose petal without the whole world watching and somehow sensing the impact. Not even the smallest action happens without consequences—for bet-ter or for worse. There's no halfway. Perhaps—and this would be best for us—we will inspire in you the courage to face up to these facts. For it takes a lot of courage to realize that every thought, every spoken word, and every action has vast and profound consequences, whether now, tomorrow, or in twen-ty years. The fate of the world lies in the hands of individu-als—of each individual.

The best thing about all this is the adventure of personal experience. With personal experience you can exchange the oppressive weight of supposition, opinion, and conviction for the comfort of knowledge and truth.

FOR EVERY ILL A HEALING HERB— A SHORT HERBAL

MEDICINAL HERBS ARE miniature power stations. There is hardly a bodily ailment, hardly an illness that cannot be relieved or healed by the leaves, flowers, fruit, or roots of a naturally occurring herb—always provided that the patient approaches the remedy and the sickness in the correct frame of mind.

Anyone who makes wise use of herbs in the kitchen is not only doing a great deal to improve the taste of the food, but is also ensuring that many illnesses are avoided. Perhaps the time has come to return to the principle of the ancient Chinese: people provided for the support of their doctors—in money and natural produce—only as long as they remained healthy. If a "lamb" in the doctor's flock fell ill, then he was released from this communal duty. In those times doctors earned their living from the *health* of those in their charge, not their illness.

A great variety of medicinal agents are contained in herbs, often in one and the same plant:

Mucilage (pectin) used against inflammations of all kinds and to heal wounds, contained for example in comfrey, coltsfoot, cowslip, cornflower, daisy, dead-nettle, marigold.

Essential oils with a variety of effects (disinfecting, stimulating blood supply, stimulating or inhibiting secretion, dehydrating), contained in thyme, garlic, yellow gentian, sage, chamomile, laurel, balm, fennel, basil.

Soapy substances (saponin) with a broad spectrum of effects, contained in (among other plants) liverwort, cowslip, birch, speedwell, heartsease, mullein.

Silicic acid for treatment of skin inflammations and mucus membrane, and to strengthen connective tissue, contained for example in horsetail, heather, stinging nettle.

Bitter substances (alkaloids, glycosides) for regulating the functioning of the stomach and intestine, releasing tension and convulsions, contained in wormwood, yellow gentian, mugwort, dandelion, sage, marigold.

Tannic acid for inflammations of the stomach and mucus membrane of the intestine, contained in (among other plants) bramble, lady's mantle, speedwell.

Salicylic acid with anti-bacterial and pain-relieving effects, contained in willow, violet, marigold.

Styptic (blood-staunching) agents contained in shepherd's purse, yarrow, mistletoe, dandelion.

Laxative agents contained in senna leaves, alder bark, common buckthorn, fumitory.

This list is far from being exhaustive, and even today new agents are still being discovered. At the same time our wonder can only grow at the unerring instinct of our forebears, who discovered the effective herb for each different illness.

After numerous shifts in medical outlook the realization is slowly gaining acceptance once more that the whole is always more than the sum of its parts; for example, that the pure active agents of a medicinal herb used in high doses are still weaker in the long run than the plant or part of a plant taken as an entity in itself.

Atomic physics has contributed a great deal to this reorientation through its recognition of the fact that the firm borderline between "dead matter" and life is merely an illusion of thinking that every single thing stands simultaneously in the closest connection with the entire universe. In the words of the nuclear physicist and Nobel Prize winner Werner Heisenberg, "We are bound to realize that what we are studying possesses all the characteristics that are normally ascribed to God."

The fact that a medicinal herb can only work in its totality is part of age-old folk-wisdom which cannot be driven into oblivion. Just as a hundred years ago official medicine thought differently from the way it does today, in a hundred years' time it will look back pityingly on current methods.

It was Indians, Egyptians, Jews, Greeks, Romans, and above all Arabs, who brought the science of medicinal herbs to a high level. At first Christianity, in its efforts to eradicate "heathen" customs, went a little too far and turned its back on large parts of this knowledge. But this was counterbalanced by the work of medically skilled monastic orders, which, circumventing official dogma, cherished the ancient lore.

We have to thank in particular the Benedictine monks, but also temporal rulers such as Charlemagne, for the revival of herbal science in the Middle Ages. Albertus Magnus and Paracelsus also helped to ensure that the classical writers Hippocrates, Galen, and Dioscorides were once more studied and taught. Paracelsus's indefatigable struggle against the materialistic view of man and disease is well-documented and is reminiscent in many respects of the feud that still persists today between natural healing and academic medicine. With the difference that today an additional tactic is pursued by the orthodox medical camp: a mixture of irony, cynicism, and ignoring the alternative view. This is the most effective method of all, for in an open contest with "drums beating and trumpets sounding" every bystander has the chance to get to know both sides very well and then decide for himself. In the long run, however, truth will prevail. Until that happens, we shall have to place more trust in ourselves than in any "authority."

The light of nature does not lie,

but the theoreticians have turned the light against nature.

If man is perverse, he will also pervert the light of nature.

Therefore seek first the kingdom of Truth,

and you will do more than has ever been done on earth.

Never doubt God, our greatest physician.

As we love him and our neighbor, so he will grant us everything

we need. But if we are idle and neglectful of love,

then even that will be taken from us which we believe to be ours.

—Paracelsus

Perhaps you will feel something is missing on the next pages: a comprehensive list of medicinal herbs with their ranges of application, or else an exact enumeration of widespread illnesses together with the herbs that are indicated for each of them. For various reasons we decided against that. For instance, herbs are only rarely suitable for patent remedies. The vast majority of herbs are helpful, using a part or the whole of the plant, in a number of different disorders; conversely, in the case of a particular illness, there is a wide variety of herbs that may possibly serve as palliative or healing remedies. There exist outstanding books on herbs to which very little need be added. What is still lacking in them, "the correct lunar timing," is something you will discover in this chapter.

When you read an herbal, you will realize immediately that many of our kitchen herbs are plants with preventive and curative effects on many illnesses—from parsley and chives to rosemary, sage, and lovage, to sweet woodruff and mugwort. They have now undeservedly sunk to the level of taste enhancers—or perhaps even lower, since chemistry performs the work of "improving taste" more thoroughly than nature. Even more surprising, however, is the fact that many plants that are considered "weeds," from stinging nettles to dandelions, also have a medicinal effect—plants, the very sight of which drives amateur gardeners into their sheds to get out their chemicals and exterminate them root and branch. What a reversal of the world! For instance, there is nothing better than a blood purification treatment in early spring using stinging nettles that have been picked at the right time. And as for the power residing in the young leaves or open flowers of dandelions: that is known to anyone whose complaints have been relieved or healed by this means.

HERBS AT THE CORRECT TIME

A great many herbs can help us to lead a harmonious and healthy daily life. The knowledge concerning the right moment to gather and store them is of great value in order to obtain the greatest possible healing power and durability. Which of these herbs do you think is more effective?

A sage seed seeks out for itself a particular place to open up, grow, and ripen. In its "correct" place it sprouts up, encounters sun, wind, and rain, struggles to assert itself, puts down deep roots in order to get to vital moisture and minerals, grows in the neighborhood of numerous other plants, adapts to the climate of radiation and all the negative influences in the environment in order to survive. This wild sage is plucked by skilled hands at just the right moment, lovingly and carefully dried or stored, prepared into an infusion for liver or gallbladder complaints, and drunk at the right moment by a sick person living in the same surroundings under the same climatic conditions as the plant itself. In other words: the sage grew *for* this suffering person.

Another sage seed grows up on a distant plantation, sown at any old time, perhaps ripening in a greenhouse, nursed, watered, and tended, treated with pesticides, rescued from weeds, putting down feeble and shallow roots, gathered at any old time and sold to a pharmaceutical firm. There, at some time or other, it is further processed and extracted, the active agents are isolated and processed into a preparation to combat liver and gallbladder complaints; this turns up at a wholesaler's and eventually reaches the pharmacies of another country and is prescribed by a doctor for a sick person. In other words, *what did this sage grow for?*

This example contains the secret of many medicinal herb experts: the effectiveness of a plant is determined by correct timing when gathering, processing, and using it, as well as the location in which it grows.

With all medicinal herbs it is important to study the active agents more closely. The unity of a plant or part of a plant should be maintained; for just as we found when discussing a healthy diet, the roughage of a medicinal herb is of great value.

However, attention should be paid to what task the plant is to fulfill: whether it is supposed to arrest inflammation, act as a laxative, or have a strengthening effect on certain organs. Every plant possesses different characteristics, different ingredients. Furthermore, not every plant is equally good for everyone. One person will not be able to take a particular herb for one complaint while for another person the same herb can bring a rapid cure for the identical complaint. Every human being reacts in a unique way, which has to be taken into account. Once the question as to which herb has been answered, then the rules for gathering it require our attention.

Rules for Gathering Herbs

The dominant principle when gathering herbs in the wild or harvesting them in the garden should be this: only gather as much as you need for your current purposes or for your anticipated winter requirements. Respect for nature and consideration for one's neighbors demand as much. Rare herbs that are protected by law must remain taboo.

Always restrict yourself to herbs that you know well and can identify with certainty. The greatest care is needed especially when digging up roots, because otherwise the plant could be exterminated at the site where you found it. A few plants should always be left behind; you should only pick the part of the plant that is needed for the treatment.

The Correct Moment

The healing power of herbs is not evenly distributed over the whole plant. Many gathering times are very unfavorable, because the active agent is currently in the flowering herb while what you need for your application is the root. It can also happen that you are collecting flowers or leaves while the healing sap is actually gathering new strength in the roots.

Often in the leaflets that come with natural products one finds the advice that variations in color or cloudiness are normal occurrences. From this one can tell that the harvests do not always turn out equally well, particularly when it is a question of cultivated herbs from plantations, where it is only rarely possible to watch out for the correct moment.

Choosing the correct time for gathering *your personal feeling* and *observation of the state of the weather* should always come first. Certainly the flower days (Gemini, Libra, Aquarius) are in general very suitable for picking flowers, but if the sun is not shining and the weather is cold, then the fact that it's a favorable moment will not help much. One should always be alert to what is and what is not appropriate and feasible on any given day. The advice concerning the correct time for gathering herbs is very valuable, but if good, dry weather conditions are not forecast, then it's pointless to collect herbs.

The Best Season
A rough guideline for the best season for herb gathering is as follows: in spring, when the plant is still young, it possesses the greatest healing power. With young plants the component substances are released more easily; with older plants often not at all (for instance silicic acid). They remain ineffective (see also page 65).

The Best Time of Day
Gather *roots* in the morning and evening.
Pick *leaves* in the late morning, after the dew has dried.
Gather *flowers* in sunshine. They must be fully unfurled, but not about to fade; otherwise their healing power is greatly reduced.
Seeds and fruit may be gathered at any time of day, because they are not so sensitive as other parts of the plant; however, one should avoid the greatest midday heat.

Position of the Moon in the Zodiac
The position of the moon in the zodiac has a significant bearing on gathering and using medicinal herbs. The relevant rule here is:

❦

A herb that is gathered for the healing or strengthening of those parts of the body that are governed by the zodiac sign of the gathering day is especially effective.

❦

Herbs gathed on *Virgo days*, for example, are especially helpful in dealing with complaints of the digestion. From herbs collected on *Pisces days* an excellent foot ointment can be prepared. The following table will make it easier for you to see the connections:

In the Sign of	*Gather Herbs For*
Aries	headaches, eye complaints
Taurus	sore throat, ear complaints
Gemini	tensions in the shoulders, lung complaints (for inhalation)
Cancer	bronchitis; stomach, liver, and gallbladder complaints
Leo	heart and circulation complaints
Virgo	disorders of the digestive organs and pancreas, nervous complaints
Libra	hip complaints, diseases of the kidneys and gallbladder
Scorpio	diseases of the sexual and eliminating organs; good gathering day for all herbs
Sagittarius	vein diseases
Capricorn	bone and joint complaints, skin diseases
Aquarius	vein diseases
Pisces	foot complaints

However, you should always bear in mind that when you are gathering herbs *the weather must be dry.* This rule is thus only of limited use, because the weather does not always play along with such precise attention to timing, and one might well have to wait weeks for the right conditions. On the other hand there are many prolonged and chronic sicknesses that frequently can be successfully treated with herbs collected during the correct sign of the zodiac. In such cases a lengthy wait is well worthwhile.

The Individual Parts of the Plant

It is easier to observe the correct moment to gather the different parts of the plant than to keep exactly to the correct sign of the zodiac, and it also produces good results.

- *Roots:* The correct moment to dig up roots is the early spring, when the plant is not yet in full growth, or the autumn, when the herb has withdrawn into itself once more; at that time the sap has descended again.

  You should always dig up roots when the moon is *full or waning*; they have more power at that time. They should not be exposed to sunlight, so the night hours before sunrise or the late evening are therefore the best times.

  The period of the *descending moon* (see Chapter 1) and the *root days* of Taurus, Capricorn and Virgo are also suitable as a gathering time; however, Taurus is not quite so good as the other two signs.

- *Leaves:* these may be gathered throughout almost the whole year, provided that the plants are young. If the plant has already been producing sap for a long time, or is already in bloom or has not been mown, it is not very suitable for curative purposes.

It is not necessary for picking to take place when the sun is shining, but the morning dew should have evaporated; so late morning is the best time.

Leaves should be gathered when the *moon is waxing*, between new and full moon; alternatively when the *moon is ascending* (Sagittarius to Gemini), or on *leaf days* (Cancer, Scorpio, and Pisces). Herbs gathered during *Scorpio* possess a special curative power. In addition they are outstandingly suitable for drying, preserving, and storing. Herbs gathered during Cancer and Pisces are better used right away. A special exception to this is the stinging nettle. This outstanding blood-purifying remedy should be gathered exclusively when the moon is *on the wane*, and nettle tea should also only be drunk during the *waning* moon. For more details about this, please refer to the end of the chapter.

- *Flowers*: Generally the most favorable gathering times are spring and summer, when the plants are in full bloom, particularly at midday. The sun should be shining, or at least the weather should be warm, so that the flowers are open and the healing force has traveled up to the blooms; withered plants are not especially suitable.

 Flower gathering should take place when *the moon is waxing or full*; alternatively when the moon is *ascending* (Sagittarius to Gemini), if the weather precludes gathering when the moon is waxing. *Flower days* (Gemini, Libra, or Aquarius) are also suitable—or simply at full moon, regardless of the zodiac sign.

 If you are gathering for winter storage then *waning* and *descending* moon are also suitable because the flowers will be more certain to dry at that time.

- *Fruits and seeds*: these should be ripe when gathered, neither green nor squashy. This is almost always only the case in summer or autumn. Dry weather is more important than the time of day; however, you should avoid the greatest midday heat.

Fruits and seeds gathered when the moon is waxing are only suitable for immediate use. For storing and preserving the *ascending* moon (Sagittarius to Gemini) is better. Good gathering days are the *fruit days* (Aries, Leo, and Sagittarius). The most unfavorable days for collecting fruit are Capricorn, Pisces, Cancer, and Virgo.

THE "MYSTERIOUS" POWER OF THE FULL MOON

Many readers may be reminded now of horror stories about witches who carry out strange manipulations by moonlight and then come home to their black cat from their nocturnal herb-gathering outings, riding on a broomstick.

What certainly is true is that the day of the full moon is an outstanding collecting time for almost all herbs and parts of herbs. Roots in particular, when gathered at full moon or when the moon is on the wane, have greater curative power than at other times. Moreover, roots—especially those that are to serve as a *cure for serious illnesses*—should under no circumstances be exposed to sunlight. At the time of full moon the visibility is just about good enough to recognize an herb, whereas at new moon you can't see your hand in front of your face. Formerly there were no flashlights, and it would not have occurred to anyone, least of all medical people, to go into the forest with a flaming brand.

The reason why cats are always appearing in witch stories is because people used to observe cats and draw useful conclusions from their behavior. Cats prefer to sleep and rest on "bad spots"— places in the house that have negative energy (such as water veins, earth radiation). In former times, wherever a cat felt at home one would never set up a workplace—even less a bed. There will be more on this very important subject later on in the book.

Thus it can be seen that many a fairy tale from olden times has its roots in concrete and sensible facts.

PRESERVING HERBS

Care is essential when preserving, drying, storing, and keeping herbs. The plants need to be put in a shady spot to dry, and they should be turned often. A natural material that is pervious to air is a suitable underlay (ideally a wooden cutting board, but paper will serve just as well). However, one should never dry herbs on any kind of plastic sheet. Nothing should be kept for more than a year, which is not really a problem since fresh supplies of plants are obtainable every year. Don't forget that one should never collect too much. Moderation, reason, and sensitivity should be the factors determining quantity.

The correct time for *storing* herbs and *filling* jars or cardboard boxes with herbs is always when the moon is *on the wane*, regardless of the date the herbs were gathered. Never put them into containers when the moon is waxing, otherwise there is a danger they might rot.

Dark jars and paper bags are the most suitable storage containers. The plants will remain nice and dry; the aroma and active ingredients will be retained. Bright light has an unfavorable effect.

Plants have different drying times. You must take care to ensure that herbs gathered when the moon is waxing undergo some of their drying process during the waning moon.

It is not necessary with every type of herb to dry its individual parts. In the case of many medicinal and kitchen herbs (such as marjoram, thyme, lovage, and parsley) it is sufficient to hang several plants upside down like a bunch of flowers in an airy place until they have dried. They can be put in containers later in the usual way. This method saves space, looks good, and the aroma creates a pleasant atmosphere in a room. Quick-drying herbs are most suited for this since there is no danger that tying them up will cause rotting.

Perhaps after all of this you will object that not everyone can go herb gathering in the countryside, or has a herb garden to call his own. It should be emphasized that plants from a florist, grocery store, or herbalist's shop also have their value, and often do a lot of good. It is only in the case of chronic, persistent illnesses that the correct moment of gathering is of special importance and should be observed at all costs.

PREPARATION AND USE

Often herbs have the best effect when eaten raw or cooked as a vegetable (sage, elderflower), as a salad (watercress, young dandelion) or a spinach (stinging nettles, wood garlic). But in addition to this there are many other methods of preparation and use, a few of which we will discuss here:

- *Teas and Infusions*: One of the most common uses for herbs. This is especially suitable for young herbs containing essential oils that evaporate with prolonged boiling.

  As a unit of measure, place as much of the dried or fresh herb as you can hold in three fingers in a cup, pour boiling water onto it, cover, leave to steep for three to ten minutes, and then strain (don't use a metal strainer). A valid rule of thumb is that the tea is ready when the herbs have sunk to the bottom; however, some herbs that contain a lot of oil will not sink even after several hours. In such cases ten to fifteen minutes is enough. The tea should be drunk immediately so that it does not lose its medicinal ingredients needlessly.

- *Boiling (extraction)*: This is suitable for plants containing curative ingredients that are not readily soluble (bitters, tannic acid), and especially for wood, roots, or stems. The boiling time is a matter of instinct; as a rule not more than 15 minutes. Some wood and roots need to be boiled for up to half an hour. Where possible avoid using pots made of steel, iron, copper, or brass.

Opinions diverge as to whether the plants should be added to already boiling water or put in cold water and slowly brought to the boil. At home I was taught the latter method, and until now I have been unable to discover any advantage in the former method.

- *Cold extraction*: Some herbs cannot stand either brewing or boiling. One puts such plants in cold water and leaves them standing overnight. In addition to this it is sometimes a good idea the next day to strain the herbs and bring them to a boil in some fresh water (not the liquid produced by cold extraction) and in this way extract the remaining medicinal ingredients.
- *Extracts*: Thicker herbal extracts with cold-pressed olive oil poured over them produce mild embrocations.
- *Raw juices*: Many herbs are suitable for crushing. However, the juices obtained do not keep and should be used at once (as a drink or perhaps as a compress, depending on the herb).
- *Tinctures*: These are thin extracts that are mostly obtained with diluted ethyl alcohol. Place a handful of herbs in dark bottles and fill them up, for example with fruit

brandy, until the herbs are covered. After storing for about two weeks in a warm place the tincture will be ready for use.

    Ointments and plaster mixtures: Plants and plant extracts can also be ground or boiled down with soft fats and made into ointments or mixtures for plasters. Anyone able to buy meat from a farmer who still raises his stock in a natural way should make the most of this and ask him for fat from a pig that was slaughtered at full moon. Perhaps the farmer will actually know that the meat is much more succulent at that time and keeps better. The fat should be rendered down at a low heat; *Virgo days* should be avoided for rendering because it will easily go moldy during that period and not keep very well. At home we add the fresh herbs to the heated pork fat (*marigolds* are especially suitable) and allow it to fry for a short time (as a rule of thumb, about as long as for a cutlet). Two handfuls of herbs to a jam jar of fat should be enough. Next let the warm fat stand together with the herbs in a cool place for about 24 hours. Warm it gently the following day until the mixture becomes fluid once more. Strain it into clean jars and store in the dark. This ointment is an outstanding remedy for various illnesses, for instance as a chest embrocation for coughs and bronchitis.

It is important that this work is carried out with patience and love, and never in a hurry. It is only in this way that the right feel can be developed for the preparation and relative amounts of herbs and fat. Always work with enamel pots and wooden spoons for stirring.

    The correct time for producing ointments is any day between Sagittarius and Gemini—that is to say during the *ascending moon*. If for reasons of time you are forced to choose another date, then you should at the very least avoid Cancer and Virgo.

Sometimes in my lectures I joke that you won't have any time on Virgo days anyway, since these are the best days for gardening tasks, such as re-potting and planting flowers and trees.

An equally good time for making ointments is at full moon. The plants then contain a maximum amount of medicinal substances. After standing for 24 hours, the ointment is poured into jars when the moon is on the wane, which guarantees that it will keep a long time.

❧ *Herb pillows*: These are an excellent thing. However, please do not use protected plants for this purpose. The herbs should be picked when the moon is waxing, and when the moon is waning they should be put into pillows of a thick, natural material (e.g. linen) and then sewn up. If they are gathered on flower days, their fragrance will give you pleasure for a long time.

The choice of herbs depends on the intended use of the pillow. Generally it is to aid relaxation and provide a pleasant aroma. Your pharmacist can give you advice and combine the various herbs for you. Even herbs that have been bought should nonetheless be processed when the moon is waning. Further uses are for rheumatism and allergies. Herb pillows can bring about considerable relief in this area.

In former times, when there were still enough ferns available, people used to line a whole bed with them. The ferns were sewn in between two sheets and this was used as an under-blanket, especially for people suffering from rheumatism. Likewise if the patient suffered from cramp at night, his pillows were filled with common clubmoss. For good reason some ferns are protected species now: however; it is possible to buy them. Of course the full moon will not have been taken into consideration as the best collecting day; but even so they will contain curative substances.

Such pillows should never be aired in damp weather. You should air and loosen up aromatic pillows when the weather is dry.

THREE PRACTICAL EXAMPLES

❧ *A remedy to purify the blood*: A great many illnesses result in "bad blood," often recognizable in blemished, unhealthy looking skin, and in the laboratory in higher than normal cholesterol and urine readings. A blood purification cure using stinging nettles, continued until the disorder has died away, can do a lot of good in such cases. Also for any healthy individual a spring cure of nettle tea will drive springtime fatigue out of his limbs. This cure stimulates the bladder and kidneys, promotes the activity of all the digestive organs, and gives the body numerous minerals and vitamins.

When the moon is on the wane (if possible in the afternoon between three and seven P.M.) drink as much nettle tea as you can (a little over four pints; for this quantity use about two heaped tablespoons of the herb). Then wait 14 days, and repeat the cure the next time the moon is waning, until the ailment has improved or disappeared. As a cure for healthy people, two periods of 14 days in the waning moon are sufficient.

The stinging nettles are also best collected when the moon is waning. Only use young leaves; naturally in the springtime fresh stinging nettles are preferable to dried ones.

If the moon happens to be in an earth sign (Virgo, Taurus, Capricorn), collect a few more nettles than you need for daily use and dry the leaves for winter. There is no need for you to carry out a full blood purification cure in winter; however, it's a good idea to have a nettle tea now and then after a substantial heavy meal (e.g. during the calorie-rich holiday period). In general earth days are a particularly suitable time to do something for your blood.

➤ *The treatment of warts:* Warts, moles, and strawberry marks should only be removed or treated *when the moon is on the wane*, regardless of the method you are using. If the treatment has not been successfully concluded by new moon, stop it completely, and don't start it up again until next full moon (often this will no longer be necessary). Treatments or operations during the waxing moon (particularly on Cancer days) can turn out very unfavorably.

The greater celandine is a proven remedy for warts. Begin the treatment on full moon day and spread fresh celandine sap on the wart every day. The sap is orange-colored and seeps out of the broken stalk. Take care: it's poisonous and must not be taken internally. Continue the treatment until the new moon, even if the wart has already disappeared before then.

Using *garlic* during the waning moon, those particularly painful warts on the soles of the feet can be removed easily. Cut a hole in a plaster the same size as the wart and stick it on with the wart protruding through the hole in the plaster. Cut a fresh clove of garlic in half, affix it with another plaster over the wart and wear this through the night. In the morning, if possible after taking a shower, remove the plaster, and repeat the process each evening with a new clove of garlic. Stop when the new moon arrives. Gradually the wart will go dark and eventually it will be a simple matter to remove it.

❧ *Weaning:* Weaning is very easily done and no medicine is needed—except if it takes place immediately after birth. In the weeks before full moon, the mother simply puts the baby less and less frequently to her breast, and she no longer drinks so much herself. At full moon she breast-feeds the child one last time and drinks very little on this day. A sage tea will further assist in bringing milk production to an end.

A FEW IMPORTANT RULES OF HEALTH

THE GREATEST WISDOM REVEALS ITSELF IN THE SIMPLE

AND NATURAL ARRANGEMENT OF THINGS,

AND PEOPLE DO NOT RECOGNIZE IT

PRECISELY BECAUSE EVERYTHING IS SO SIMPLE AND NATURAL.

—Johann Peter Hebel

IN THIS CHAPTER you will encounter a few more rules for health, not all of which are connected with the lunar cycles. They are based like all the other rules on firsthand experience and long years of observation. If you are looking for proof, you will have to try things out for yourself, calmly and patiently. This is the only proof that can be offered and that has any validity. Doctors and statisticians, however, will not have much difficulty checking the correctness of these rules if they use their patients' records to compare the varying success rate of cures with the cycles of the moon. The reaction "I've never heard of such a thing, so it cannot be true" may not be very helpful; however, it is understandable enough: only a few hundred years ago people were tarred and feathered for maintaining that silk comes from caterpillars. Everyone "knew" that silk was made by angels.

Here once again are the basic characteristics of the two phases of the moon:

THE WAXING MOON

supplies, plans, takes in, builds up, absorbs, breathes in, stores energy, gathers strength, and is conducive to rest and recovery.

THE WANING MOON

washes out, detoxifies, removes, sweats out and breathes out, hardens, dries, and is conducive to action and the expenditure of energy.

It is certainly difficult in modern times to adapt to this sort of rhythm. Almost all sequences of events, rituals, and customs in private and professional life no longer make any allowances for the inherent impulses of nature. This is how stress arises in its manifold forms, so often compelling us to forget and ignore natural signals, natural instinct, and common sense.

Already a great deal would be gained by recognizing that health-damaging stress is in the majority of cases created by ourselves—that it is the consequence of too much or too little volition at the wrong moment. It often arises when inwardly or outwardly one is not up to a *self-imposed* task or if one is inwardly resisting it.

Our body reacts if we *continually* force it to ignore its natural rhythms and needs. Not at first, when we are young and can shake off negative effects like water off a duck's back, or can simply take an aspirin. But gradually these many little impulses add up until they lead to an illness—the tip of an iceberg—whose actual cause can only be traced with great difficulty. To turn a German saying on its head: "What lasts a long time finishes ill."

For that reason it must be pointed out again and again that this book is not a cure-all full of instant remedies. The effects of going against natural rhythms are slow to make themselves felt, and likewise living in tune with these rhythms will be slow to show positive effects. If one sits back quietly once a day and briefly reflects on which activities in one's daily life can be harmonized with the lunar rhythms, then one is bound to find solutions. We are not talking in terms of a feat that has to be achieved, but instead the result of an observation that opens up the way to "correct" action, all by itself, little by little, organically, definitely not from one day to the next.

There is at least one thing you can do for a start: all strenuous daily work and hobbies (for nowadays the latter often degenerate into hard work) that are *not* subject to a fixed timetable, should be postponed a little until the moon is in its waning phase. Not all at once: slowly, little by little, closely observing the effects of this action.

Nothing is more convincing than your own personal perception. Practically all tasks about the house, for example—those that are connected with cleaning, flushing out, getting rid of dirt, dust, and damp—are much better kept for the two weeks of the waning moon (see Chapter 5). When you feel how pleasant it is no longer to restrain your strength so much when the moon is waning, and when it is waxing to slow down more, to gather your strength, to prepare and plan—then you will begin to wonder how you were able to manage for so long without using this knowledge and why you had never noticed it before.

THE TOPIC OF OPERATIONS

Concerning the tricky subject of operations—surgical incursions into the body—a slightly more detailed discussion is needed. It is too important a question to be passed over in silence.

☽

This applies to surgical operations of all sorts with the exception of emergency operations: the closer to full moon the more unfavorable the moment. The actual day of full moon has the most negative effect of all. Given the choice, one should operate when the moon is waning.

Everything that puts a special burden or strain on those parts of the body and organs governed by the sign through which the moon is currently moving has a more harmful effect than on other days. Surgical interventions should therefore be avoided during these days if at all possible.

☽

Every surgeon will make this discovery, or may even already have accumulated parallel experiences: complications and infections are much more frequent on such days, and healing and convalescent phases last longer. Toward full moon there are often instances of severe bleeding that is hard to staunch.

Hippocrates (460–370 B.C.) explicitly formulated this in his journal: "Do not touch with iron those parts of the body that are governed by the sign through which the moon is passing." What he meant was that a doctor should not carry out any surgical operations on regions of the body that are governed by the current sign of the Zodiac. Which parts of the body are influenced by each sign of the zodiac can be found in the tables in Chapter 1 and at the end of this chapter. To take an example: on Pisces days operations should not be carried out on the feet; there should be no heart operations on Leo days, and so on.

Perhaps you will ask: what about the negative influence if the Leo days fall at the time of a heart operation arranged for the (favorable) waning phases of the moon? In such a situation the basic rule is this: the favorable influence of the waning moon is stronger than the negative influence of the Leo days. To stay with this example, here is a sequential list of the favorable and unfavorable influences on a heart operation:

Most unfavorable:	full moon in Leo
Very bad:	waxing mood in Leo
Bad:	waxing moon in another sign
Fair to medium:	waning moon in Leo
Good:	waning moon in another sign

Two central questions arise if one has accumulated experience of the validity of these cycles, or simply takes them on trust:

❧ *How can a surgeon in a private practice or hospital, whether as a director or an employee, integrate these rules in the running of a present-day clinic?*

Well, where there's an insight a will can emerge. And where there's a will there's a way.

❧ *How can a patient persuade his doctor to accept his own suggestion for an operating date?*

It is only in rare cases that one can go to him and base an explanation on these rules. And often it is the "practical business constraints" of the hospital or clinic that dictate the date of an operation. The final part of this chapter on health is devoted to this important point. Perhaps the thoughts and suggestions contained in it will help you not only to have your own way, but also to play a part in gaining for this knowledge the consideration that it deserves.

An Important Health Factor: "The Right Place"

℃

In every house, in every apartment there are good and bad places, regardless of what is actually in these places— whether it is a wall, table, chair, bed, or kitchen countertop.

℃

The capacity to distinguish such places one from another is developed to varying degrees in each person. As a rule, however, this sensitivity is greater in infancy and youth than in adults. The individual reaction is also different: some people spend years sleeping on a bed that is on a "bad place" without getting ill, while others become restless and nervous after sitting on a bad spot for a few minutes.

It has yet to be established *exactly* what determines the quality of a place. Certainly radiation of various types is involved—subterranean water veins, earth radiation, and the like. On the other hand there also seems to be little inclination on the part of empirical science to make a thorough investigation of phenomena that, given a modicum of good will, can be demonstrated with the greatest of ease. As long as we have a situation where any scientist instantly loses his reputation the moment he turns his attention to this subject, things will stay like this for some time to come. On the other hand precise research using conventional methods is very difficult. One of the most important reasons for this is that experienced dowsers and diviners are unlikely to make themselves available for such inquiries. They know that the presence of even one person who has doubts about this art and its value is enough to distort the results of a survey. Consequently in fact the only dowsers that offer their services to science are those who, to put it mildly, overrate their own capacities to a certain degree.

Formerly the phenomenon of the right place was well known: in ancient China no house was ever built before the ground had been minutely investigated. The Chinese were also the first to set down in writing their experiences applying this knowledge. Our ancestors used a whole array of tools to identify good and bad spots: divining rods, pendulums etc., as well as closely observing the plant and animal world. From this they discovered that many animals are definite detectors of the quality of a place: cats, ants and bees, for instance, are "ray-seekers": they prefer places that are bad for human beings. Ants and bees always build their nests at the intersection of two water veins. The fact that storks and swallows are widely held to bring good luck is perhaps connected with the fact that they only nest where the surroundings are largely radiation-free. Birds and also dogs, horses, and cows belong to the ray-fleeing group. Wherever they settle is also a good spot for us.

Many parents will have noticed this: some babies twist and turn in bed, cry a great deal, and often end up in the morning lying in a corner of the crib. Many children often cannot stand being in their own bed at night; they slip into bed with their parents or with a brother or sister. School children who sit for a whole year in the same bad place often lag behind in their work for no apparent reason, whereas up to that point everything was going well. Sometimes parents set up a very expensive and tasteful child's room with a desk in it, only to find that the child still comes to the kitchen to do his homework. Generally this is a first sign that the child's desk is in an unfavorable place.

In the adult world, too, many things can be observed that are connected with good and bad places:

Formerly it was known that in certain farms, no milkmaid could stick to it longer than a couple of months, that the farmer or the farmer's wife always died young there, almost as if there was a curse weighing down on the house. In most cases this had to do with bad sleeping and working places.

Perhaps you have noticed how some housewives stand at an angle or at a distance from their kitchen table, or that there are chairs in the living room that inexplicably remain empty, or that there are certain places in your apartment where you regularly become tired or restless. Many an otherwise able and popular teacher suddenly gets a "bad" class, with which he simply cannot get along—"cannot get on a firm footing"—because his chair is in the wrong place. Sometimes he unconsciously copes with the situation by walking up and down or continually sitting on the desk instead of behind it.

Unfortunately our feelings concerning a particular place are not always a sure sign of its quality. Some people have become so accustomed to the negative energies of bad spots—perhaps because their bed has been over a bad spot for years—that they are actually magnetically attracted to "bad" places.

However, the insight that there are "good" and "bad" places and the manner of identifying them is extremely important when it is a question of our health. Sitting or sleeping for years on the wrong place can be responsible or partially responsible for lengthy, chronic illnesses, chronic headaches, tiredness, and the like to such an extent that one is forced to what is perhaps a somewhat drastic conclusion: *It is almost suicidal to come home after an operation or a protracted illness and then sleep in the same bed in the same position.* Any person suffering from chronic health disorders should have his sleeping or working area investigated by people who are skilled in this art.

Of course you will now be asking what you *yourself* can do in order to determine the quality of a place? Unfortunately there is no patent formula. If you have begun to suspect and have reason to suppose that you yourself or someone in your family may be sleeping or working in a bad place, try out a rearrangement of the furniture. Usually a distance of about two yards away from the old spot is sufficient.

Only a few people are fortunate enough to know a good dowser or diviner in their neighborhood. For those who would like to try out and develop *their own* abilities as a dowser, we recommend the following book on dowsing and the use of the pendulum: *The Pendulum Kit* by Sig Lonegren, Eddison Sadd Editions, London.

HOW TO GIVE UP A BAD HABIT

This section can be dealt with in a single sentence:

☾

A good starting point for giving up bad habits is the day of new moon, best of all the new moon in March, when the sun changes from Pisces to Aries (though this is not so much better that you should wait for months to make your good resolution).

☾

However, the subject of "good resolutions" deserves to be discussed in greater detail. The day of the new moon may be the most favorable moment, but before a "bad habit" can be given up a remarkable hurdle stands in the way.

Before you make the decision—"I'm going to give up smoking [or drinking]," "I'm going to stop bearing grudges," "I'm going to take better care of my children," "I'm going to stop eating so much," "Starting today I'm going to do more exercise," and so forth—you should ask yourself two questions:

- ✦ Is the fault that I wish to eradicate really a fault?
- ✦ What is my reason for getting rid of it?

Apropos of the first question, a tiny fable: A monkey scooped a fish out of the water and laid it on a branch. "What are you doing that for?" asked another monkey. "I'm saving it from drowning," was the answer.

Are you sure that the thing you are trying to remove really is a fault? Is it really a bad habit? Perhaps with your desire to change yourself, you are just obeying a social convention that has nothing to do with your real nature. Perhaps you are a strong, temperamental person who constantly forces himself not to face up to his real nature out of a misconceived consideration for others. All of us have a strange "monkey" in us that only too often tries to pull the inner fish out of the water in order to save it. Often bad habits are only "bad" because we have been trained to describe them as such. Or else they are misguided powers that only need to be reoriented in order to be valuable and useful for us, and thus for our fellow human beings.

Perhaps this will sound a little provocative: if you find a *rational* answer to the second question about your motive for giving up a bad habit, then you should abandon your purpose. The only thing that really counts is your inner decision, your clear inner intention *without* any if or but or because. If you decide "because it's healthy, because I want to prove something to my mom, my boss, my partner, myself, everybody else, because it'll make me better-looking, because my partner is giving it up as well, because it'll make me a better person," then you have laid the foundation for the failure of your intention. Even if, by summoning up all your strength, self-discipline, and severity with yourself, you should succeed in giving up the bad habit it will either come back again or else turn up somewhere else—perhaps even in a much more harmful form.

On Repentance

Repentance means turning back or giving up completely something that was of powerful attraction. Pleasure gained through repentance is in most cases as bad as the original offence, and no permanent improvement can be expected by those who pride themselves in reformation. The repentance of the ignorant is when people feel strong reactions to giving something up, or seek forgiveness for something. There is a higher form, the repentance of the Wise, which leads to greater knowledge and love.

—Pahlawan-i-Saif

Hard as this may seem, often the deeper reasons for giving up bad habits are vanity, fear, pride, and greed. So, what have I achieved if I get rid of the fault? I have augmented my vanity, fear, pride, and greed have given them more strength than they had before. And as to what the consequences of this are, there is no need to tell you. Simply look around you.

☽

Thus, if you wish to give up a bad habit, look it quietly and calmly in the face, study it from all angles. And then decide to give it up (or not). Why? Because that is your will, and that's that. Full stop. Then choose the day of the new moon to carry out your decision. It can help you.

☽

THE RHYTHM OF THE BODILY ORGANS
THROUGHOUT THE DAY

In the course of twenty-four hours each organ in the body passes through a high phase, in which for two hours it works especially well and efficiently, and then, as can be seen in the following table, immediately after that it takes a "creative break" for two hours.

Every mountaineer knows that if he gets up at three A.M. he is off to a much better start than he would be at five A.M. At three A.M. his lungs work particularly well for a period of two hours. A good start makes it much easier for him to bridge over the drop in energy after five o'clock—by then he will have got into his stride. On the other hand if he starts at five in the morning he will have a struggle to get going.

Parents know very well that if they manage to get their children to bed before seven o'clock, they often go to sleep without any problem. But if the seven P.M. line is overstepped by much, it becomes twice as difficult to lull them to sleep. Between seven and nine in the evening the circulation is working at its best. At this time the body isn't thinking of sleep.

Almost everyone will have noticed that around one o'clock there is often a falling off of performance, especially after lunch. The small intestine, which bears the main burden in many digestive processes, tries to come into its own. It works especially well at this time and wants the rest of the body to take a break. Its activity is controlled by the vegetative (unconsciously functioning) nervous system, which cannot tolerate any form of stress. Thus we see that the "siesta" of southern climes finds an echo in the daily rhythms of the organs.

THE RHYTHM OF THE BODILY ORGANS THROUGHOUT THE DAY

Organ	High phase	Low phase
liver	1 A.M.–3 A.M.	3 A.M.–5 A.M.
lungs	3 A.M.–5 A.M.	5 A.M.–7 A.M.
large intestine	5 A.M.–7 A.M.	7 A.M.–9 A.M.
stomach	7 A.M.–9 A.M.	9 A.M.–11 A.M.
spleen and pancreas	9 A.M.–11 A.M.	11 A.M.–1 P.M.
heart	11 A.M.–1 P.M.	1 P.M.–3 P.M.
small intestine	1 P.M.–3 P.M.	3 P.M.–5 P.M.
bladder	3 P.M.–5 P.M.	5 P.M.–7 P.M.
kidneys	5 P.M.–7 P.M.	7 P.M.–9 P.M.
circulation	7 P.M.–9 P.M.	9 P.M.–11 P.M.
general energy accumulation	9 P.M.–11 P.M.	11 P.M.–1 A.M.
gallbladder	11 P.M.–1 A.M.	1 A.M.–3 A.M.

You can make use of this knowledge in the following manner: if you know the high phases of the various organs, you will be able to take medicines or flush out poisons—or take any other measure that serves your well-being and health— at the right moment throughout the day, regardless of the position of the moon.

For example, drink a tea to purify the blood between three and five in the afternoon, catch 40 winks between one and three (take a nap in the office), don't eat breakfast after nine in the morning, smoke and drink less between one and five in the morning, and so on.

Observe yourself, watch, be aware, take down notes: experience is better than information. Information is only a tool. The hand using the tool needs practice as well. And the same goes for the heart that moves the hand.

GOING TO THE DENTIST

The work of dentists is also influenced by the position of the moon. If any dentist is interested in checking out this influence then a simple test will suffice. First he should fish out from his patient records all cases in which a filling, crown, or bridge inexplicably fell out too soon, say within three years of being inserted. Using calendars he can then build up a checklist: on the left he can enter all cases in which the insertion took place when the moon was waxing, and on the right when the moon was waning. The results will speak for themselves.

☽

Whenever possible the fitting of crowns and bridges should take place when the moon is waning.

☽

Of course it is not always easy to keep to the right date, to say nothing of adapting a dental practice to the lunar cycles. However, perhaps you will find one or other of the suggestions at the end of this chapter helpful.

THE INTERRELATIONSHIP BETWEEN THE
POSITION OF THE MOON IN THE ZODIAC
AND BODILY HEALTH

THE TWO- TO THREE-DAY sojourn of the moon in each of the 12 signs of the zodiac awakens different forces that are perceptible everywhere in the animate world and also have a marked effect on our bodies. The principle, starting point and effect of these forces are not especially difficult to describe; but on top of that they possess a kind of "coloring" which isn't easy to put into words—something that leaves its mark on our mental and emotional temperament, like a musical chord that sounds from far away and can be heard by those with ears to hear. On the following pages you will find a summary of the individual impulses and their implications for health, ordered according to zodiac sign.

Zodiac sign	Body part affected	System
Aries	head, brain, eyes	sense organs
Taurus	larynx, speech organs, teeth, jaws, neck, tonsils, ears	blood circulation
Gemini	shoulders, arms, hands, lungs	glandular system
Cancer	chest, lungs, stomach, liver, gallbladder	nervous system
Leo	heart, back, diaphragm, circulation, arteries	sense organs
Virgo	digestive organs, nerves, spleen, pancreas	blood circulation
Libra	hips, kidneys, bladder	glandular system
Scorpio	sex organs, ureter	nervous system
Sagittarius	thigh, veins	sense organs
Capricorn	knee, bones, joints, skin	blood circulation
Aquarius	lower leg, veins	glandular system
Pisces	feet, toes	nervous system

The basic rules are as follows:

- Everything that is done for the well-being of those parts of the body and organs governed by the sign through which the moon is currently passing is doubly useful and beneficial—with the exception of surgical operations.
- Everything that puts a special burden or strain on those

parts of the body and organs governed by the sign through which the moon is currently moving is doubly harmful. Surgical operations should be avoided during these days if at all possible, with the exception of emergency operations.

If the moon is waxing as it passes through the sign, then all measures taken to supply nutrient materials and strengthen the region of the body governed by the sign are more effective than when the moon is on the wane. If it is waning, then all measures taken to flush out and detoxify the region in question are more successful than when the moon is waxing.

The actual form of therapy used—medicine, massage, gymnastics, water therapy, etc.—does not matter so much as the ultimate intention that is being pursued by these means.

In the waxing moon
October to April
In the waning moon
April to October

ARIES

Coloring: Aries is energetic, at times impatient, "banging its head against a brick wall." At this time unseen chains rattle audibly and are less willingly carried. Things get going and the way straight ahead seems the best.

With the zodiac sign Aries the bodily influences start up in the head region. Anyone who is especially susceptible to migraine will often feel it keenly during the two or three Aries days in the lunar month.

I have often been able to observe that many people, especially women, are plagued with violent headaches on these days. Frequently they themselves contribute toward the outbreak of headaches through their behavior prior to the Aries days. They have a talent for putting off important matters, household chores, and appointments shortly before the Aries days, until precisely on the Aries day itself it all comes crashing down on them. Observe yourself and try to keep the Aries days as free of stress as you possibly can.

Another good measure for avoiding migraine is to drink a lot of water on Aries days and go without coffee, chocolate, and sugar. As is so often the case, this piece of advice will only be useful for those people who have already learned to pay heed to their own body's signals. Anyone who has mastered this language is able to form a clear picture of everything that helps or harms his or her body.

There are thousands of medicines, teas, and ointments, thousands of good and well-intentioned pieces of advice, which might possibly help with one and the same disturbance in our well-being. There's nothing to be said against that, but if I "listen in" to myself then a single one of these remedies will be sufficient, namely the one that actually helps me. No medicine is only good or only bad. What will help ultimately depends on the individual human being. But for that it is essential for me to have a "feeling" for myself; the opinion of experts is often not enough. Unfortunately this feeling is often only gained through illness and suffering. "Whoever has no time for his health will have to find time for his sickness." In particular, chronically ill people would do well to learn from their illness, instead of placing themselves in the hands of medical science and having themselves "treated." The insight that the entire body needs to be treated and that a different way of life is necessary is better than just struggling against symptoms.

With this attitude one can avoid headaches on Aries days, thereby achieving much more than someone who without any insight drinks a gallon of water and waits to see if it helps. It won't do any good. This remedy may have helped friends of ours often enough, but ultimately it is only a suggestion. It can't be made into a general rule.

The sign of Aries also affects the eyes and the brain. In principle there is nothing good or bad about Aries days for the head region. It all depends what you do. Eye compresses for inflamed or exhausted eyes on Aries days are bound to be effective.

Herbs that are known for their effectiveness with headaches and eye complaints (eyebright, etc.) develop greater strength when gathered during Aries days. When stocking up, one should pick them when the moon is waning and also dry and store them during that phase. One old and effective remedy for exhausted and strained eyes is to moisten one's closed eyelids with one's own saliva, in the morning before eating, and only when the moon is on the wane.

Injuries to the eyes (which cannot always be avoided) and overexertion are more harmful at this time than in Libra, to give one example. If you possibly can, do your eyes a favor today.

Especially critical Aries days occur in March, April, September, and October. Everyone who frequently suffers from headaches or who is sensitive in the head region should arrange for these days to be as peaceful as possible. Likewise operations on the head should be avoided. The Aries days in October are especially bad because they fall directly at full moon.

TAURUS

In the waxing moon
November to May
In the waning moon
May to November

Coloring: "Realism" is the order of the day, material security becomes a virtue. Persistence is easier, thoughts and reactions slower.

Obstinacy. "The white horse of the Arabs is as swift as the wind, but the camel trots day and night through the desert."

With the entry of the moon into the sign of Taurus the neck region of the body is more strongly affected. Again this is to be understood in this way: good influences are especially good, unfavorable ones especially bad.

For weeks a young man goes riding in his convertible in beautiful, warm weather and enjoys the airflow. And then one day, literally "out of a clear blue sky" he gets a stiff neck, is reduced to giving himself neck compresses all day long, and feels like an old man.

Or you suddenly get a sore throat and notice at the same time that friends, neighbors, and colleagues are going around with croaking voices and scarves about their necks, even though colds and inflammations of the throat are not always infectious. In many cases this is Taurus "kicking in." Which doesn't mean of course that one is bound to get a sore throat at this time. But there definitely is a greater danger of inflammations of the throat.

The information concerning the forces prevailing in the different signs of the zodiac can give you valuable tips about precautionary measures. Anyone who has ever taken a tea for hoarseness or inflamed tonsils on Taurus days knows just how effective a simple tea can be. Other medicines for inflammations of the throat are also especially effective during these days.

Taurus affects the organs of speech, the jaws, teeth, tonsils, the thyroid gland, the neck, vocal chords, and ears. Giving a speech on Taurus days can be agony for the inexperienced and may end in hoarse croaking.

Particularly on cold Taurus days the ears should not remain unprotected. At this time they are more sensitive to drafts and noise. An eardrop of St. John's wort oil now and then on Taurus days can often prevent earache, especially when the St. John's wort flowers used for the oil were gathered during Taurus.

In the waxing moon
December to June
In the waning moon
June to December

GEMINI

Coloring: The mind becomes active and versatile, moving in leaps and bounds. A breath of wind can deflect it from its course. The forces branch out and penetrate into every corner.

Rheumatic gout in the region of the shoulders responds particularly well at this time to suitable ointments, possibly produced from herbs that were gathered during Gemini and Taurus. On the other hand wearing clothing that is too light in cool weather can cause your body to be unpleasantly conscious of itself.

Gemini days are always an occasion to do some good to the shoulder area; well-directed exercises can work wonders and be a treat for your shoulders. However, you will not necessarily be spared from stiff muscles afterwards. In any case this is probably a good sign, for that is how the body signals that it is busy with detoxification.

The lungs are influenced a little by the Gemini days, even if they are much more strongly affected by the sign of Cancer. Properly directed breathing exercises would be very useful at this time.

Those suffering from rheumatism sometimes have difficulties during the Gemini days, but the reason for this often lies in the fact that the weather in Gemini tends to be very changeable. We are not just talking here about clearly noticeable switches between sunshine and rain or vice versa. Changes of climate are affected in a variety of ways. Indeed the Bavarians could tell us a thing or two about this: they know what a strong *Föhn* wind can mean for their well-being. Warm, katabatic winds with sonorous names (Sirocco, Khamsin, Chinook) that burden the circulation are found all over the world.

CANCER

In the waxing moon
January to July
In the waning moon
July to January

Coloring: Feelings gain depth, but also weight. The inner becomes more colorful that the outer. The ground shakes. It becomes easier to make sacrifices. Dense, extensive growth.

The force that prevails during the Cancer days often shifts our general state into one of slight restlessness. Much more strongly than in the other signs of the zodiac, the influence is predominantly felt in the chest. The Cancer sign also "rules" the liver, and often staying up all night is enough to make one feel totally shattered the next day because the liver has had too much to do. If you happen to be susceptible to complaints of the liver, gallbladder, lungs, or chest, you should take advantage of Cancer days to do these organs some good. The stomach, too, occasionally plays up during Cancer days (wind, heartburn). A light diet is advisable.

From the month of July to the following January Cancer days always occur in the waning moon, and then for the next six months in the waxing moon. You will recall that when the moon is on the wane the system is flushed out; when it is waxing it is supplied with as much goodness as possible.

This means that in the case of the stomach and liver, healing or expelling poisons has more chance of success in the period from summer to winter than from winter to summer.

Anyone who suffers from rheumatism should not hang bedding outside to air during Cancer (a water sign). The damp remains in the bedding, and one feels chilly all night.

LEO

In the waxing moon
February to August
In the waning moon
August to February

Coloring: Muscles swell, determination reigns, people "take heart." Limits lose their sharp outlines somewhat and appear to be more easily surmountable. Pleasure in risk, fire that dries out.

The Leo impulse makes the blood circulation "sing." It is more active now than on other days. The back sometimes hurts more, and not infrequently the heart plays up a little. Sleepless nights can cause a lot of trouble during Leo; however, by the time Virgo comes it's usually all over.

Everything that could overstrain the heart and circulation should be avoided if possible during Leo. Of course we aren't talking about the normal physical activities of healthy people. People with heart problems can sometimes already sense during the sign of Cancer that Leo is on the way. Such people especially should steer clear of strenuous journeys or undertakings at this time. Many an inexperienced hiker puffs his way to the summit during Leo, even though he has problems with his circulation or heart. Particularly during Leo days he should refrain from making any demanding trips.

Although the sign of Virgo is responsible for the digestive organs, anyone thinking of taking curative or tonic measures should start now. In addition, Leo is a very good day to collect herbs that have a curative effect on the heart and circulation.

VIRGO

In the waxing moon
March to September
In the waning moon
September to March

Coloring: The logically arguable end justifies the means. Small, hesitant, methodical steps, almost pedantic. First investigate, then act. Things are separated and split up with the object of developing them.

The particular force of the Virgo days makes itself apparent in the digestive organs. Sensitive people in particular often have problems with their digestion at this time. A correspondingly wholesome diet is recommended during these days; at the very least one should give up heavy or fatty dishes.

Herbs gathered during Virgo have a favorable effect not only on the stomach, but also on the blood, nerves, and pancreas. In particular a blood-purifying infusion, such as stinging nettles gathered in Virgo, is bound to have a good effect. The winter store should not be laid down until September (young plants that have grown again after mowing), when Virgo appears once more in the waning moon. Such a tea is especially good for an enlarged pancreas.

LIBRA

In the waxing moon
April to October
In the waning moon
October to April

Coloring: The artistic rules, but so, too, does indecisiveness. Tactful sensitivity, without much punch. Swinging this way and that, till equilibrium is achieved.

The hip region, the bladder, and kidneys can make themselves particularly noticeable during the Libra days. It is easier to get bladder or kidney inflammations at this time. Take special care to keep the area of the bladder and kidneys warm. Sitting on stones or wet grass in Libra is asking for trouble.

One useful measure is to drink a great deal between three and five in the afternoon, in order to rinse the bladder and kidneys thoroughly.

Special exercises for the hip region are particularly helpful at this time.

Often I am asked the best time, in terms of the position of the moon, to carry out a hip operation. The correct moment for this is when the moon is waning. In the months from April to October the star sign of Libra never occurs in the waning moon, i.e. both conditions are favorable. In addition, the star sign that rules the part of the body under consideration should never be the current one in the calendar. If you should only have time for an operation between October and April, then you should avoid the star sign Libra in the waning moon.

SCORPIO

In the waxing moon
May to November
In the waning moon
November to May

Coloring: "Opportunities are precious, and time is a sharp sword." Acceptance is difficult. Energy goes deeper, bores its way down and searches. Darkness beckons.

No zodiac sign has as strong an effect on the sexual organs as Scorpio. As a precaution hip baths using yarrow can be of assistance at this time in a great many female disorders.

Mothers-to-be should beware of any exertion on Scorpio days, because miscarriages can happen more easily, especially when the moon is waxing.

The ureter, too, is especially sensitive during Scorpio and repays positive influence. Cold feet and failure to keep the region of the pelvis and kidneys warm can easily lead to inflammations of the bladder and kidney. Anyone who suffers from rheumatism shouldn't air bedding outside in the Scorpio days (water sign): moisture will remain in the bedding.

All medicinal herbs gathered during Scorpio are especially effective. Fetch all your herbs home by May/June to make a pillow, then they will give you pleasure for many years. However, the actual filling of the medicinal pillows should not take place in Scorpio, because a water sign is not very suitable on account of the moisture.

Sowing medicinal herbs is also good during Scorpio days.

SAGITTARIUS

In the waxing moon
June to December
In the waning moon
December to June

Coloring: The future seems more important than the present and past, the great more important than the small, bringing together more important than splitting asunder. Magnanimity reigns, but so, too, does pathos. The stride lengthens.

Sagittarius affects the hips, pelvis, ilium, sacrum, and thighbone. The sciatic nerve, veins, and thighs make their presence especially strongly felt on Sagittarius days. On top of that, there are often pains in the small of the back down to the thighs, because during Sagittarius, as in Gemini, the weather can easily switch. Massages do a lot of good and loosen up tense muscles. On the other hand a body that is out of shape will really feel the effect of long hikes on the thighs.

So one shouldn't overdo it during Sagittarius and go on long hikes without first training. Anyone who picks on Sagittarius to take the kids on their first major mountain hike, or perhaps even forces them into it, could very well put them off hiking for a long time to come.

CAPRICORN

In the waxing moon
July to January
In the waning moon
January to July

Coloring: The air becomes transparent, thinking clear and serious, straightforward, somewhat inflexible. The goal seems more important than the way there.

An excessive strain on the skeleton in general and the knees in particular can have serious consequences during Capricorn days. Just as in Sagittarius, after a long break, or if you are a beginner, you should not start out on mountaineering or skiing trips. Surgeons and orthopedic specialists know precisely when the moon is passing through Capricorn: they are able to enlarge their stock of experience of knee operations. Football or soccer players with meniscus problems should under no circumstances overdo it at this time.

With every movement heavy demands are put on the knees. Knee poultices are particularly useful either as a precaution or a cure during these two or three days. One can also do some good at this time for other bones and joints. In addition these days are very suitable for any kind of skin care (see also Chapter 5).

In the waxing moon
August to February
In the waning moon
February to August

AQUARIUS

Coloring: The mind invents capers, intuitive thoughts get heard. Shackles are not tolerated—not even imaginary ones.

Aquarius affects the lower leg and ankle joint. Inflammation of the veins is not uncommon during Aquarius. Now is the time to put some ointment on your lower legs and rest your legs in a raised position.

Anyone who is inclined to get varicose veins should avoid long periods of standing on these days; even a longish stroll around town can be a nightmare on Aquarius days. Taxi drivers generally have more to do at this time.

Operations on varicose veins should not be carried out during Aquarius.

In the waxing moon
September to March
In the waning moon
March to September

PISCES

Coloring: The common good comes before individual advantage. Borders become blurred, it is easier to take a look behind the scenes, and the world is tinged with fantasy. Rigid points of view are avoided; plenty of bowing and scraping.

Aries began the cycle with a force influencing the head; Pisces ends it with the feet. If you follow up the cycle of impulses and gradually perceive them within yourself, you will no longer need to be constantly on the lookout. The course of a single month is sufficient in order to give the body consciously what it needs—from top to bottom—and to pay special attention to specific weak points.

Pisces is the best time for footbaths and the treatment (but not the surgical removal) of corns. During Pisces days warts on the feet can be treated with considerable success. However, it is essential to look out for the waning moon: if the moon is waxing it may well be that after treatment you suddenly have five warts instead of three.

One peculiar feature of the Pisces days is this: everything that you allow into your body during these days—alcohol, nicotine, coffee, medicine—has a much stronger effect than at other times. Presumably this is because the meridians of all the internal organs terminate in the feet, and thus react with special sensitivity on Pisces days.

THE CORRECT WAY TO DEAL WITH DOCTORS

A GREAT DEAL of pioneering work remains to be done before medicine will be able once again to make use of the slow rhythms of nature on a broad front. This task will not lie so much in the area of research and discovery, for the knowledge already exists to a large extent. Instead it will be a matter of overcoming resistance— one's own as well as that of those around us. This requires courage and patience.

Of course, even from an organizational standpoint it is impossible to fix the times for operations exclusively on the most favorable dates. But in many cases—for instance in serious operations, after inexplicable treatment failures, when trying to avoid major scars—one could easily keep to the most favorable time. In such cases doctors could for once apply the rules. Certainly one thing that would be helpful for doctors would be to check from their own patient records the dates of past treatments and operations—

one of the best methods there is to find confirmation for the validity of these rules.

There are already many pioneers: doctors and practitioners who are perfectly willing to observe these rules and whose experiences have made them immune to any kind of resistance. They are no longer surprised if they are asked to carry out a blood test on a particular date, or to postpone appointments. They are still the exception, but it is a very promising start.

So, what is to be done when you yourself have gradually gained confidence in these rules as a result of personal experience, but your doctor as yet knows nothing about the rhythms and wishes to perform an operation at an unfavorable time or carry out some other inappropriate measure? Again it depends on your feeling.

If you sense that your doctor is ready to listen to your reasons for a postponement, then you could simply read him the precept of Hippocrates: "Do not touch with iron those parts of the body that are governed by the sign through which the moon is passing."—or else you could refer him to a section in this book that applies to your case. Such doctors are in the majority, so the risk is certainly justifiable. However, if he refuses to postpone, that is still no reason to look for another doctor. Ask him for a precise explanation for his refusal and only then should you make a decision. But you should not immediately accept "difficulties" in arranging appointments as a reason. They are often just a pretext to avoid having to go into the question of natural rhythms in more detail.

However, if you are certain that your doctor is not likely to summon up any understanding for the real reasons why you wish to alter an appointment—unfortunately that type also exists—then it isn't such a bad idea to think up a few plausible excuses. There's no point having a guilty conscience about it: after all, a valuable asset is at stake, namely your health. Bear in mind that all a doctor can ever do is help you to help yourself. Deep within yourself you know what is good for you and what is not. You often even know exactly what the cause of your complaints is, because we generally reap what we ourselves have sown. It is only that many of us have allowed ourselves to be seduced into looking the other way, or are simply too idle and place all responsibility for our own illness in the hands of the doctor. With such an attitude we are asking too much of any doctor. He will not really be able to help you, or at best only in the short term.

Let us cite here from our book *Moon Time: Retaining and Regaining your Health in Tune with Natural and Lunar Rhythms*:

> To retain or regain your health, throughout an entire lifetime, with all its ups and downs, is in fact neither difficult nor complicated; nor does it need to be expensive or laborious. For a long time large areas of modern science, in particular orthodox medicine and psychology—closely interwoven with politics, religion, economics, industry and advertising—have effectively conspired to convince us of the contrary and to make us believe that only the specialist with his secret knowledge and secret language is able to heal or to point the way to a healthy and meaningful life. They pursue this goal in part consciously, in part unconsciously, and for a variety of motives: in order that their throne remains untouched, their largely superfluous products (goods or ideologies) remain marketable, and above all we, the consumers and recipients of their "favors," remain more easily amenable, subordinate, and dependent.
>
> We are pleased that so many people today wish to strike out in another direction. We want to help along this slow process of rethinking in every possible way. In so doing we shall have recourse to things that have always worked: to the basic materials and cornerstones of a healthy, dynamic, and worthwhile life. We want to bring back to life all that is natural, plain and simple, without indiscriminately throwing overboard the genuine blessings that the modern age has brought us. In any case the future is not going to leave us any other choice in the matter—so why not take the first steps willingly and joyfully?

Sensing, watching, experiencing is the key to many things in nature that science cannot unveil—at least not with its restricted methods and from the high horse it loves to ride.

We shall have achieved everything we wanted if we only succeed in awakening your memory: If you remember that you possess everything you need—all means, powers and capacities—in order to live a life that is really worthy of the name. Life! Let us not confuse a meaningful life with that chaotic alternation that has been drilled into us—of expectation and disappointment, numbness and pain, anxiety and relief, pleasure and frustration, stress and idleness.

Not for a moment is man a foreign body on the earth and in the universe. Nature is not engaged in any struggle with humanity, but instead gives it everything it needs, as long as each individual learns to live in friendship with himself and with nature. This friendship can never be one that is prescribed by law. It is your own personal achievement, your own personal decision. The choice is always yours, no matter how hard people try to persuade you to the contrary. All of us—human beings, animals, plants, stars, planets, sun and moon, you and us—we are all in the same boat. And the only purpose of our lives consists in waking each other up and being there for each other—no matter how long humanity still needs in order to realize this. The best medicine for man is man.

The medicine of the future will be a mutual enrichment, a confluence of the most ancient healing methods and the best of modern medical science. An art in which magic and medicaments, loving touch and scalpel strokes, healing mental activity, prayer and meditation, after centuries of unnatural separation, finally meld into a unity that once again sees humanity as a whole. This is the only possible way.

Inner instinct, observation, and direct experience showed our forefathers the way to natural and lunar rhythms, to a knowledge that deserves our grateful acceptance. We proposed to acquaint you with a portion of this knowledge. May it serve you well.

T H R E E

Lunar Rhythms in the Garden and the Countryside

A MAN IS BORN GENTLE AND WEAK.

AT HIS DEATH HE IS HARD AND STIFF.

GREEN PLANTS ARE TENDER AND FILLED WITH SAP.

AT THEIR DEATH THEY ARE WITHERED AND DRY.

THEREFORE THE STIFF AND UNBENDING IS THE DISCIPLE OF DEATH.

THE GENTLE AND YIELDING IS THE DISCIPLE OF LIFE.

THUS AN ARMY WITHOUT FLEXIBILITY NEVER WINS A BATTLE.

A TREE THAT IS UNBENDING IS EASILY BROKEN.

THE HARD AND STRONG WILL FALL.

THE SOFT AND WEAK WILL OVERCOME.

—Lao Tsu

THERE ARE MANY reasons in gardening, agriculture, and forestry for returning to the observance of the phases of the moon and the position of the moon in the zodiac. One of the most important is that with the aid of lunar rhythms it is possible for us to move away from the exaggerated use of chemical pesticides, insecticides, and fertilizers and find our way back to a natural and dynamic balance in nature. The gardening and agriculture of the future will have no other choice, because one can't exploit nature indefinitely. So why shouldn't we start now?

A short while ago I was flying from Hamburg to Munich. The weather was perfect and I had a window seat. I couldn't keep my eyes off the ground ten miles below me: it seemed to me there wasn't a single spot that wasn't utilized, cultivated, built up, and furrowed with roads. And even if I saw a largish, continuous stretch of woodland, there would be bound to be some gravel works or other building sunk right in the middle of it. The thought came to me: how lovely it would be if we could learn once more to treat nature in such a way that this view would only awaken pleasant feelings.

An unsprayed apple, grown in harmony with natural rhythms, is unlikely to win a prize in an agricultural show these days. And yet visual effect is in almost every respect a question of fashion and taste, and is thus a transitory phenomenon. There's an old saying that "Many people are hungry because they do not like the color of the plate on which the food is served." A wild apple may not be conventionally beautiful, but it contains a hundred times more life and strength than any forced plantation apple buried under a layer of wax.

In our age "healthy" is often synonymous with sterile, or germ-free. How can our immune system ever develop its power of resistance if all its work is taken away from it and it is denied the necessary hardening process? That is just as true of plants (vegetables, cereals, fruit) and the vital strength in them that we wish to use for ourselves.

So many digestive disorders nowadays, and many other illnesses that follow in their wake, may be attributed to this "healthy" diet of inwardly dead foodstuffs. Germ-free food is sterile, infertile food. Of course, in the case of some diseases it may well be appropriate, but for a healthy person it paves the way to sickness.

WITH TOTALLY UNPREDICTABLE results for the entire cycle of nature, millions of dollars are spent today on research into breeding and genetic engineering with the purpose of transforming plants in such a way that, on command, they will do what they would have done in any case, given the correct choice of moment for planting, nurturing, and gathering.

This situation is reminiscent of the good intentions of nutritional scientists at the turn of the century. They had observed that in the process of feeding, certain substances enter the body and are subsequently expelled again unchanged. "They are therefore superfluous," such was the judgment; they declared them to be "dead weight" and began to rid foodstuffs of them and produce food that was "ready-to-eat." The consequences are well-known.

The Carrier Parrot

A man crossed a carrier pigeon with a parrot, so that their descendants would be able to speak the message instead of having to carry it on a piece of paper.

But the bird that resulted from this experiment took hours to complete a flight that normally would only have taken minutes.

"What kept you?" asked the man.

"Well," said the bird, "it was such a nice day that I decided to go on foot."

THE PRICE OF SCIENTIFIC ADVANCES

Science and technology have led us to the conviction that practically all problems can be solved through their agency, even problems that but for them we would never have encountered. The successes were really enormous: crops increased, pests disappeared, unlimited opportunities seemed to open up. Only gradually were people forced to recognize that exploitation is not the ultimate wisdom.

This book is intended to help wisdom and reason come into their own once more in the sphere of gardening, agriculture and the countryside in general.

It is not a matter of cursing the chemical and food industries because of poisons and chemicals, for these industries fulfill many useful purposes in our lives. However, it is entirely up to the individual at what point he places his faith in chemistry and uses chemical products. The expression, "What can the individual do about it?" is just an excuse for inactivity and resignation. A single human being with good will and good thoughts is capable of providing an entire town with inspiration and the courage and strength to go on living, even if he never appears in public (perhaps often because of that).

If you are one of those people who at the very least do not want to poison their own fruit, vegetables, and cereals, then you will find many suggestions on the following pages that will make it easy to give up using these substances. The fact that it is possible to garden and farm without using poisons and without the manipulations of genetic engineering, and yet produce higher, equal, or only slightly lower yields and a much higher quality of harvest, is something that a great many people know today—including those whose direct concern it is.

There are so many proofs: fruits that only carry within them the strength of the sun which gave them their color, cereals that let us taste the meaning of harmony between heaven and earth, vegetables that carry this harmony into our bodies, earth that willingly bestows these gifts on us for centuries on end, without fertilizers and other poisons.

Perhaps you have one or two experiences of your own that come to your mind. Almost everyone who has anything to do with gardening and country life has experienced things that on closer inspection simply cannot be explained. At various times, under completely identical conditions, we sow, plant, water, transplant, fertilize, harvest, and store—but with totally different results. Sometimes the lettuce forms a nice head; sometimes it bolts flowers and seeds and cannot be used. Sometimes a farmer harvests the most wonderful turnips, while his neighbor, using the same seeds, and with the same weather conditions and soil, is dissatisfied with the result. Then again one's own crop is attacked by pests, while the neighbor's remains untouched. Or a small strip at the edge of a cornfield flourishes much better than the remaining area. Sometimes the part of the potato plant above ground grows splendidly, but the crop itself remains undeveloped. At other times the plant looks stunted, and yet it yields the most enormous potatoes. Sometimes the cherry jam lasts for years; then again the finest fruit can quickly go moldy, even though everything was preserved under the same conditions.

So the weather, the seeds, or the quality of the soil often have to be invoked as a way of making the inexplicable at least comprehensible. In many cases that may well be true, but much more frequently the reason is simply that attention was not paid to the correct timing of the task in question.

Perhaps you have already noticed that in a lettuce or a cabbage plot *all* the plants shoot up and bolt or *all* the plants form a head. You never find both conditions simultaneously in the same bed. It is almost never the seed that is at fault: that much is certain.

Of course, simply giving up spraying and fertilizing and just following the rhythms of the moon will not bring about the desired results. Our soils have become much too spoiled for that; the change calls for patience. Instead you should proceed slowly: the knowledge that people have been testing and using for thousands of years before you will be your reward. None of it is "new"; it is just that technical progress has seduced us into supposing that we can afford to push this valuable inheritance into the background or even let it sink entirely into oblivion. Have courage: it doesn't cost anything, and in any case the work on the fruit, vegetables, and cereals has to be done. While you are sowing, planting, or harvesting, pay attention to the signs of the zodiac and the phase of the moon. Then in due course you will be pleasantly surprised by your success in every respect.

You need not despair, either, if deadlines or weather conditions spoil your plans and prevent you from observing the "correct" times: you will discover that there are several alternatives for every task in the garden or the field—times that are also suitable or almost as suitable. However, in every case you should take care to avoid the unfavorable times.

Of course we cannot discuss every plant in detail here: that would be missing the point. But the principles can easily be applied to other tasks in the garden and the field.

My idea as to why I want to write this knowledge down is simple. It is so that you may obtain, if that is your desire, a knowledge that can accompany you your whole life long, without having to be forever looking things up in textbooks and guides—a knowledge that becomes second nature to you. Perhaps my personal outlook will be of further assistance to you in seeing the advantages of a thorough rethinking of how to do things. I also enjoyed my early days in Munich to the fullest, and very quickly forgot my responsibility toward the natural world, because of course "you can buy anything you want." Prices seemed so low to me in comparison with income. It is all too easy to get the impression that physical labor is no longer worthwhile, since fruit and vegetables are "cheap." However, when I came back home after a long time and ate the local lettuce, I noticed an enormous and unmistakable difference. But at that time this was not yet sufficient reason for me to return to natural ways. I had to fall ill first. Even then I tried everything else before I fully realized: I can't and won't go on living like this. I learned once more to take responsibility for my own body, and understood that I can only eat good vegetables if I actually have the possibility to get hold of healthy vegetables. The wheel had turned full circle and I accepted the years of thoughtlessness as a learning process. So all that is needed is experience and clarification. That is why it is not difficult either for a town dweller to realize after a certain amount of observation that a short-term success is no success at all. It is essential for us to learn again how to accept responsibility and not let ourselves be blinded out of sheer laziness.

The following table summarizes once more the most important impulse characteristics of the zodiac signs in all work in the garden, on the land, and in the countryside—the effect on the different parts of plants, the day quality (see Chapter 5), and the ascending or descending force inherent in each sign.

THE IMPULSE CHARACTERISTICS OF THE ZODIAC SIGNS

Sign	Symbol	Plant Part	Element	Day Quality	Ascending/ Descending
Aries	🐏	Fruit	Fire	Warmth	◡
Taurus	🐂	Root	Earth	Cold	◡
Gemini	👯	Flower	Air	Air/Light	◠
Cancer	♋	Leaf	Water	Wetness	◠
Leo	🦁	Fruit	Fire	Warmth	◠
Virgo	♍	Root	Earth	Cold	◠
Libra	♎	Flower	Air	Air/Light	◠
Scorpio	♏	Leaf	Water	Wetness	◠
Sagittarius	♐	Fruit	Fire	Warmth	◡
Capricorn	♑	Root	Earth	Cold	◡
Aquarius	♒	Flower	Air	Air/Light	◡
Pisces	♓	Leaf	Water	Wetness	◡

◡ = Ascending Moon
◠ = Descending Moon

Every sign of the zodiac has an effect on a different part of a plant. By means of this table and the calendars included at the back of the book, you will be able to interpret correctly the tips that are given in the following chapter and adapt your gardening work to these rhythms. By taking into account the most favorable times for the various tasks in the garden you will be able to avoid many negative influences, and your successes will be a source of pleasure for you.

SOWING AND PLANTING

THE MAIN WORK both in the garden and in the field generally begins in the spring with turning over the soil, followed by sowing and planting. The correct timing of these tasks is extremely important for the growth and ripening of plants and for their resistance to weeds and pests.

In Chapter 2 we discussed how greatly our bodies and our health are affected by the varying impulses of the waxing and waning moon, the full moon and the new moon, and the position of the moon in the zodiac. In addition to that, in the plant kingdom the varying forces of the *ascending* and *descending* moon also have a part to play and can be used in many ways—often as an alternative when the most favorable time for a particular task in the garden or the field has to be missed.

The ascending and descending moon are terms that refer exclusively to the position of the moon in the zodiac; they are independent of the moon's phases. An important time for a great many planting activities is the approximately 13-day period of the *descending moon*. Descending Moon: *Gemini, Cancer, Leo, Virgo, Libra, Scorpio (Sagittarius)*. Ascending Moon: *Sagittarius, Capricorn, Aquarius, Pisces, Aries, Taurus (Gemini)*. *Gemini* and *Sagittarius* are nodal points at which the ascending and descending forces each change direction—similarly to the way in which the forces realign themselves at full and new moon. For that reason Gemini and Sagittarius cannot be tied down so exactly to descending and ascending impulses.

And so when in the following pages we talk of the descending moon, you must not forget that this has nothing to do with the waning moon. However, if you look closely at the calendar at the back of the book, you will see that both rhythms can overlap and influence each other.

THE CHOICE OF MOON PHASE

Our bodies are tuned, when the moon is *waning*, to giving, expending energy, activity; when it is *waxing*, to breathing in, planning, conservation, and gathering strength. With the soil the exact reverse is the case:

℄

When the moon is on the wane the sap runs to the roots; the soil is receptive and breathes in. But when the moon is waxing the sap climbs more, and growth above ground, breathing out, predominates.

℄

This "reversed" rhythm forms the basis of many rules for work in the garden and on the land. However, before we come to the rules for sowing and planting, it will definitely be useful briefly to give a tip about digging over a newly laid-out garden plot in spring, since this always precedes the planting work.

☾

In the spring dig over each bed three times. The first time when the moon is waxing in Leo, then in Capricorn with the moon on the wane, and finally a third time—again preferably when the moon is waning. Other than that the timing of the third digging is no longer so important.

In spring, appropriately enough, the zodiac sign Leo always occurs when the moon is waxing, and Capricorn always when it is waning. Why this rule works so well will be explained in more detail later. For the moment, weeding and digging over with the waxing moon in Leo brings into action all the seeds of the weeds buried in the soil; everything sprouts and germinates. The same action with the moon on the wane in Capricorn ensures that the weeds disappear and almost nothing returns because there are no more seeds in the ground. If you keep to this rule for digging over the soil, you will have created the best conditions for profiting from the tips that now follow.

☾

The basic rule for planting and sowing is as follows:

☾

Plants and vegetables that grow and flourish above ground should be sown when the moon is waxing, or alternatively when it is descending.

Vegetables that grow below ground will thrive if the waning moon is taken into account when selecting the sowing or planting day. If this time is not practicable, then an alternative time can be chosen when the moon is descending.

☾

With the aid of the calendar at the back of the book you will have no difficulty in selecting these moon phases and at the same time paying attention to the zodiac sign.

THE CHOICE OF ZODIAC SIGN

When it comes to choosing the correct sign of the zodiac, it depends what you want from a plant—which part of the plant is to receive the best chances of development.

- Tomatoes, for example, are *fruit*, not leaves, roots or flowers. You should therefore choose a fruit day for planting or sowing tomatoes—Aries, Leo, Sagittarius.
- *Leaf vegetables* (spinach, leeks, etc.) are best planted or sown when there is a leaf day in the calendar—Cancer, Scorpio, Pisces. When planting or sowing lettuce, however, there should also always be a waning moon.
- The same principle also applies to *root vegetables*, for example celeriac, carrots, onions, and radish. Here you are hardly likely to set store by pretty flowers or lushly burgeoning foliage. And so you will choose a root day—Virgo, Taurus, Capricorn.

  An exception here is the potato: although the waning moon is the correct time for planting, this should not take place too close to new moon, but shortly after full moon.
- For *flowers* and most medicinal herbs a flower day is best—Gemini, Libra, Aquarius.

When you have thoroughly grasped these principles it will no longer be difficult to create a garden planner for the whole year. Of course constraints of time and weather do not always allow one to hit on the right day. But it is easy to ensure that all the various influences do not have a negative effect—there is still plenty of lee-way, as you will discover.

On the other hand, fanaticism and over-meticulous adherence to the instructions given here will not produce good results. "Too much of a good thing" is just another way of saying "bad." Anyone who has nature for a teacher knows that there is no such thing as 100 percent perfection. It would be wise to resign yourself from the start to a certain amount of natural wastage, especially if one has to deal with "crop failure" or weeds and pests. All creatures in the community of life in which we live are bound to take a few knocks. Not every garden pest is pestilent, not every weed is an "anti-plant."

WATERING AND IRRIGATING

On the subject of watering and irrigating, here is what is possibly a rather provocative piece of advice, at least to the ears of many a passionate gardener: it is sufficient if the seed stock is well-watered at the outset. If there happens to be a period of drought at the time, then one can go on watering for a few more days; but that should definitely be the end of it. *In moderate climates additional watering is utterly pointless. In arid climates, you will find that you can save up to 70 percent of your water.*

Nowadays the soil of many gardens and fields is regularly watered, regardless of the natural conditions. This spoils the earth and makes all the plants lazy and listless, the roots grow shallow and no longer reach deep into the ground, fertilizer is washed away, the quality of the harvested produce is lifeless. In the natural rhythm of rain and drought, both soil and plant "wake up," have a good stretch and begin to breathe. Such a plant knows that every drop counts, and it catches up on what it needs. Its inner strength is different, and so is that of its fruit.

However, it would be a mistake, trusting nature and the above advice, immediately to stop this supplementary watering. The soil has to become slowly accustomed once more to the natural situation. Just like a muscle that has become flabby through misuse: first there comes the training, then the aching stiffness, then the strength—in that order.

Houseplants and balcony plants, on the other hand need to be watered, though not as often as is frequently the case. Houseplants should preferably be watered on *leaf days* (Cancer, Scorpio, Pisces), ideally with calcium-free rainwater. Perhaps this piece of advice will astonish you or even strike you as cruel, for leaf days only turn up at intervals of six to eight days. And yet: watering only on these days is sufficient (with the exception of some exotic plants). Plants that have a high water requirement should be watered several times a day, possibly on all two or three of the leaf days.

> *Even if I go away on a two-week journey, I don't need anyone to come round and water my houseplants for me. If I water them generously for the last time on a water day, so that if possible there's still some water in the base plate, all my plants will hold out. You should accustom your plants slowly, not abruptly, to this new rhythm. Exceptions to this are some very thirsty houseplants and garden plants, such as tomatoes, which need more frequent watering.*

At the very least you should give up watering on *flower days*. Pests often spread on plants that are watered on flower days (Gemini, Libra, Aquarius), lice in particular. Putting houseplants out in the open with the good intention of exposing them to the rain can have equally unfavorable effects, since the leaves often cannot stand direct watering.

CROP ROTATION AND PLANT COMMUNITIES

In vegetable growing the *rotation of crops*, the alternation of the species grown, and the choice of *plant neighborhood* are of particular importance. For gardeners this is self-evident; and there is information about it in many gardening books—plants that mutually foster one another and protect each other from pests, unsuitable plant communities, and much more. However, beginners will find one or two suggestions here.

One particularly favorable crop rotation is one in which vegetables and arable crops are cultivated that grow above and below ground level in annual alternation. Within the vegetable plot itself, biological gardeners take care to place plants with shallow roots next to plants whose roots go deep. Since the harvest times are different, the plant with the longest ripening period ends up having the most room, because the other vegetables have in the meantime been harvested.

Particularly favorable plant communities
carrots next to onions   lettuces next to radish
tomatoes next to onions   peas next to celery
tomatoes next to parsley   potatoes next to cabbage types

Favorable communities
Cucumbers go well with:
onions, runner beans, celery, beetroot, parsley, lettuce, kohlrabi, cabbage varieties, dwarf beans

Potatoes go well with:
spinach, dwarf beans, kohlrabi, dill

Celery goes well with:
dwarf beans, spinach, onions, runner beans, tomatoes, leeks, kohlrabi, cabbage varieties, cucumbers

Parsley goes well with:
tomatoes, onions, radishes, cucumbers

Tomatoes go well with:
celery, spinach, onions, parsley, cabbage types, kohlrabi, lettuce, leeks, dwarf beans, carrots

Spinach goes well with:
tomatoes, runner beans, strawberries, kohlrabi, carrots, potatoes, cabbage varieties

Lettuce goes well with:
onions, tomatoes, runner beans, dwarf beans, radishes, dill, peas, cucumbers, strawberries, carrots, cabbage varieties, leeks

Onions go well with:
tomatoes, strawberries, cucumbers, parsley, lettuce, kohlrabi

Strawberries go well with:
carrots, leeks, cabbage varieties, radish, lettuce, spinach, onions

Particularly unfavorable plant communities

beans next to onions	parsley next to lettuce
cabbage next to onions	beetroot next to tomatoes
potatoes next to onions	tomatoes next to peas
red cabbage next to tomatoes	peas next to beans

TRANSPLANTING, RE-POTTING AND CUTTINGS

Perhaps the list of good plant communities will have inspired you to put one or the other plants in your garden. For this task, too, there is a correct time.

☾

Transplanting a plant should take place when the moon is waxing, or alternatively when the moon is descending (Gemini to Sagittarius).

☾

Plants that are moved to another place or another pot at this time quickly grow new roots and thrive marvelously. Especially with older plants, and above all with older trees, it is important to pay close attention to the time of transplanting. According to an old saying, "You don't transplant an old tree." At least as far as real trees are concerned, that is not so: if you are using the time of the *descending* moon, then *Virgo days* are the best; at that time even a fairly old plant or an old tree will put down roots again. However, the season of the year should also be taken into consideration: that transplanting should take place either in spring or autumn is, one would hope, self-evident.

For cuttings, too, the period of the waxing and descending moon is favorable. They grow in quickly and in a short time develop new root hairs. Again the Virgo days are the most suitable. However, when planting cuttings in autumn you should look out for the waning moon.

COMBATING WEEDS AND PESTS

HERE ARE TWO brief pieces of information on this extremely important subject, in order to bring home to you the full importance of the problem (both from the *Süddeutsche Zeitung*, April 25, 1991):

> *Two pounds of triazine, a herbicide that is sprayed in incredible amounts (recently banned, but even the substitute materials are not exactly suitable as a sauce for potato pancakes) costs about $30.00 in the shops. In order to remove the same amount of triazine from our groundwater requires 2200 pounds activated carbon costing $5000.00, not counting the cost of removing the contaminated carbon, which also has to be rendered harmless."*
>
> *In 1940 farmers used very little insecticide. At that time pests destroyed about 3.5 percent of the harvest. Today a thousand times as much pesticide is sprayed. One would have thought that this quantity would be enough to finish off the very last cabbage white. Wrong: crop losses have currently climbed to 12 percent.*

If every manufacturer of time bombs such as this had to bear the cost of cleansing the environment of his poison, then the world would look very different. The old wisdom about natural rhythms would not have been lost, since the necessity for applying it would have continued to be felt. The tips that follow for avoiding and getting rid of pests and weeds will cost you nothing—other than a little patience.

We have already mentioned that many plants designated as "weeds"—dandelions, stinging nettles, daisies, celandines, and many others—are in almost all their parts most valuable medicinal herbs for the widest variety of ailments. At the same time, when they decompose, their great powers contribute toward the reestablishment of biological balance in a soil that has been exhausted.

In the same way, pests are often actually *beneficial*. Perhaps not for us, if we measure everything by the yield of the harvest or the beauty of the harvested fruit; but for a large number of animals—birds, beetles, caterpillars, rodents, and many other "creatures great and small." Each of these animals is a link in an endless chain, a spiral slowly turning into the future, to which we have given the names nature and evolution. Certainly nature can dispense with one or other species of plant or animal, as it has done many times in the past, and allow it to die out. But we humans cannot do so. With every exterminated species of animal and plant, there dies a piece of ourselves, of every single one of us. Until finally nature will dispense with us.

In spite of all that, so many garden lovers go into a panic at the sight of a dandelion that they dash into the shed and rummage around for the chemicals. It is this attitude that has contributed to the fact that the earth in private gardens is many times more poisoned than the ground used for agricultural purposes, even for monoculture farming. Of the 30,000 tons of pesticide in 1,724 different products with 295 poisonous ingredients, which land every year on German soil alone (and finally end up in the earth, in the groundwater, in our muscles, skin, and entrails) 2,000 tons are sold to small-time gardeners and gardening enthusiasts—mostly in order to keep lawns in "decent condition." This percentage applies worldwide!

However, anyone who does not wish to wipe nature out but to live in harmony with it should first and foremost, on sighting pests, to ask him- or herself the question: *Are they really "pests"?*

And when, using moderation and common sense, you have answered the question as to the nature of the pest, and have come to the conclusion that you want to do something about it, it is then time for a second question: *What is the cause of the infestation?*

In the answer to this is often concealed the appropriate measure needed to get rid of the nuisance, or at least effectively avoid its reappearance the next year. There are many possible reasons for a massive attack of pests, and it is certainly not easy to determine the exact cause.

Did I make a mistake in cultivation and care?
Is it possible that I chose an unsuitable soil?

The answer to these two questions can already help us move forward a great deal.

Prevention is Better than Cure

As we have already described, *fruit sequence* is a good preventive measure against a massive infestation of pests. Vegetables growing above ground should follow vegetables growing below ground, and vice versa.

From the table at the start of this chapter you can read that every sign of the zodiac has an effect on a particular part of a plant (Aries—fruit, Taurus—root, etc.). If, for instance, you repeatedly tend or water a vegetable patch when the influences are unfavorable, you are setting up a breeding ground for unwanted vermin.

Even in the domestic realm, for instance with house and balcony plants, you can observe that the plants get lice if they are often watered on flower days. The best time for houseplants to get water is on leaf days (Cancer, Scorpio, Pisces).

The best way of preventing the massive occurrence of pests is to plant and sow at the right moment, taking into account the influence of leaf, fruit, flower, and root days on flowers and plants.

Fruit Aries, Leo, Sagittarius   **Flower** Gemini, Libra, Aquarius
Root Taurus, Virgo, Capricorn   **Leaf** Cancer, Scorpio, Pisces

Sometimes the weather can wreck these calculations; but at the very least planting, sowing, and tending should not take place on a day that is actually unfavorable.

COMBATING PESTS

As every farmer and gardener knows, the correct plant community can help a great deal in keeping pests away at the very outset. Nowadays this is called "mixed cultivation." It is an immense advantage if plants can help one another to keep the pests in check.

Here are a couple of tips for dealing with the most familiar garden pests. When in the following list only plant names are given, then the planting or sowing of this plant in the vicinity of the infested growth is indicated. With these remedies, you should take care to plant all *herbs* when the moon is *waxing*, and all *bulbs* when the moon is on the *wane*.

When it is a question of *extracts* that directly help to combat pests, then it is best to proceed as follows:

Before full moon, place two large handfuls of the plant in question in 2.6 gallons of cold water; allow the extract to stand for twenty-four hours and then pour it *undiluted* on the root area, into the soil around the trunk of the infested plant (**not** on the trunk, stem, stalk, leaves or flowers). If it is to be applied when the moon is waning, you should allow the extract to stand for twice as long. Do not throw the remaining extract away: when diluted it will serve as a good fertilizer for days.

Against	Helpful
cabbage whites	peppermint, sage, tomatoes, thyme, mugwort
aphids	ladybirds, nasturtium (esp. under fruit trees), extract of stinging nettle
mites	raspberries
sawflies	tansy
flea beetles	elder-flower extract, wormwood, peppermint, onions, garlic, lettuce
ants	lavender, lamb's lettuce, tansy, dead fish (buried)
mice	garlic, crown imperial, ribbed melilot
mildew	garlic, chives, basil
carrot fly	onions, sage
fungus	chives, field horsetail
mold	bulbs
moles	when the moon is waxing, open up the hill and expose the hole, either by hand or using a harrow

If planting and tending times are taken into account, but pests still occur in large numbers, then there are some more tips concerning how to let the phases of the moon work for you in combating them.

With one or two exceptions the following may serve as a rule of thumb:

For all steps taken to combat vermin, the waning moon is appropriate.

Vermin that live in the soil are best dealt with on a root day (Taurus, Virgo, Capricorn).

Combating pests that live above ground is especially effective when the moon is in Cancer, but Gemini and Sagittarius are also suitable.

Sometimes the only thing that helps is a thorough cutting back of the plant. It is essential that this is done with the waning moon in the fourth quarter, or, best of all, exactly at full moon. In most cases the plant will then recover.

Perhaps at this point you expect a detailed list of instructions about which measures are best suited for a direct attack on pests— i.e., when the plant is already infested. But, for one thing, different types of treatment are effective with different types of plant and pest. It would be superfluous to enumerate them all here; and there are no patent remedies. And, for another thing: the best pest control is patience.

This book could help to bring about a gradual shift in thinking, away from the quick fix and back to using preventive measures and acting with moderation and practical commonsense. No *remedy* will ever solve a problem, whether it affects your pot plant or your family, profession, or daily life, if the thinking and feeling that reaches for this remedy is not in harmony with the laws of nature and if it is not guided by love and reason.

In the case of your plants: follow the indications given in the list above and in the years to come pay attention to the correct plant community; then you will generally not be tempted to reach for poisons.

A sensible approach to pests requires close observation, first and foremost. It is only when one can recognize and admit the true reason for an infestation that it is possible to take the correct action. Then you will no longer need to fight against the pests; instead a solution will occur to you that doesn't allow the pests to appear in excessive numbers in the first place. You should never waste your energy in fighting, not even in the garden.

Combating *snails and slugs* in the garden and on the land is an exception: the *waxing moon in Scorpio* is the best time for this. Fortunately nature has so arranged things that Scorpio generally occurs during the waxing phases of the moon in spring, exactly when slugs and snails are launching the attack.

Collect as many *eggshells* as you possibly can (the shells of boiled eggs are not suitable) crunch them up small when the moon is *on the wane* (when the moon is waxing the shells do not become crumbly and sharp-edged, but remain stuck to the inner skin of the egg). Then when the moon is waxing scatter the fragments around the plants and all over the plot. Of course the slugs and snails that have already crawled into the area have to be gathered up first. The sharp edges of the shell fragments act as an effective deterrent to the delicately skinned creatures.

It is essential that the moon is waxing when the shells are scattered, because otherwise the next rain will wash them into the soil. When the moon is waxing the earth does not absorb so much moisture and solid material stays lying on the surface. After some time the shells disappear into the ground (which can have the useful side effect of making the soil more limy); but by then the danger of infestation from snails is generally past.

However, in the invasions of slugs and snails in recent years, even this otherwise very effective remedy failed: then the only solution was to collect them up when they all came out in the rain. Even so, this is no reason to withhold this valuable tip from you. If there is serious danger of infestation, repeat the remedy the following month when the moon is in Scorpio.

Other suitable means for dealing with slugs and snails are spreading wood ash and sawdust, or setting up a plant community of garlic, sage, and nasturtium—to name a few examples. Also, planting marigolds around your garden beds acts as an efficient defense.

Furthermore, slugs are a real treat for some of their natural enemies such as certain duck species and in particular toads and frogs. But these latter animals are only at home in gardens that are free of poison, and for that reason they cannot simply be released. If the climate pleases them, say for instance they are attracted by a small pond, then they will come along of their own accord, even in the town. On the farm a wet meadow or a little stream is often enough to attract them.

If you wish to release frogs artificially, pay close attention to the sign of the zodiac and the day of the week. Whether the moon is waxing or waning is not so important in this case; but if the option is yours, set them loose when the moon is on the wane. However, the choice of the correct zodiac sign is very advantageous: it should not be Cancer, Leo, Taurus, or Aries. The frogs would not feel at home and would disappear again after some time, or even die. The other signs are more neutral and more suitable for such purposes. They should not be set loose on a Tuesday or a Thursday. These days are unsuitable for releasing animals of any kind (for instance after buying them, or after moving to a new house).

The hedgehog, too, is a natural enemy of slugs and snails; it eats them in large quantities. A natural garden with an autumn heap of brushwood is an enticing proposition for our prickly friend. The best time to pile up the brushwood is when the moon is *waning*: then it will stay nice and dry. This does not mean that the raindrops somehow make a detour around the heap, but instead that the hedgehog's nest beneath it will stay drier. Likewise autumn leaves raked together in a pile are an important factor enabling the hedgehog to survive the winter without coming to harm. The leaves should also be raked together when the moon is on the wane, and preferably during a dry sign (i.e. not Cancer, Scorpio or Pisces).

One last remark here: The best preventive measure against snail and slug invasions is to adhere to what we said about excessive watering.

COMBATING WEEDS

Every soil suffers if plants are cultivated on it in monoculture; that is to say, if there is always only one species of plant growing on it at one time. Bacterial life sickens, the soils become tired and poisoned, the animal and plant life in the soil deteriorates, until gradually no more viable crops can be harvested without the use of fertilizers and pesticides. The ensuing soil exhaustion is not just the result of a shortage of minerals, but is also caused by exudations from the roots of the plants being cultivated. Oats, for example, make the soil acid.

Concerning "companion plants" in monocultures (also described as "weeds"), an astonishing fact has been observed that was also known in the past to a few biologists and agricultural experts: often arable crops and weeds enter into a kind of symbiosis to maintain the quality of the soil. Charlock and wild radish, for instance, the companions of oats, de-acidify the soil and counteract the acidifying effect of the oats.

For research purposes, it is certainly interesting to note the following: there are indications that damage to health caused by a one-sided diet of cereals or other arable crops grown in monoculture can be healed precisely by those very plants that appear in conjunction with the crops in question.

You should bear these observations in mind when taking action against weeds. Perhaps this will even be transformed into worthwhile activity if, for instance, you gather dry nettles in order to make use of their great curative powers.

Of course not every weed is a medicinal herb, and there are often good reasons for wishing that once a plant has been weeded or pulled up it will never return. And so here is a helpful tip:

☽

The right moment: for pulling up weeds the most suitable time is when the moon is waning, best of all in the sign of Capricorn (Capricorn occurs in the waning moon from January to July).

☽

However, you should take care not to damage useful plants, because they can be destroyed just as easily.

We have already acquainted future "moon gardeners" with the old trick of taking advantage of the days when the moon is waxing in Leo, which are unfavorable for dealing with weeds. During Leo all kinds of weeds shoot and sprout whenever they are touched (see Chapter 1). Simply hoe over the newly laid out plot in Leo when the moon is waxing. Even the most delicate seeds will open and can then be weeded when the moon is on the wane in Capricorn—after which the plot will present a weed-free appearance for a long time to come.

In autumn all the plots should be left with a final weeding when the moon is waning. This is a good preparation for the coming year.

An especially favorable day is June 18th up until noon (until 1 P.M. all other summer days). All shrubs and weeds that are removed during these few hours will not grow back; even the roots will rot away. You will hear of one or two other rules like this that are not dependent on the phase of the moon, particularly in connection with wood-cutting. They cannot easily be explained, and can only be proven by trying them out for oneself.

CUTTING PLANTS, HEDGES AND TREES

RULES FOR CUTTING BACK PLANTS

PRUNING IS ONE of the trickier tasks in the garden: all too often we learn by experience that the same expenditure of effort and expertise produces totally different results. One time the plant shoots up; then on another occasion it becomes stunted, spreads out over the ground, or even withers completely away.

☾

The right moment: cutting back a plant should take place when the moon is waning, or else when it is descending (Gemini to Sagittarius).

☾

Plants and trees do not come to any harm if they are cut back when the moon is on the wane, because the sap does not escape. They cannot bleed to death, as the sap is descending.

PRUNING FRUIT TREES

Pruning fruit trees and shrubs is an important, annually recurring task. However, many garden-lovers, including the "pros," have from time to time had bad experiences with this. In some years it works, whereas in others it's a case of Murphy's Law. And no wonder, for this is a job that requires somewhat closer attention to correct timing.

☾

The right moment for pruning fruit trees and shrubs is when the moon is on the wane, preferably on a fruit day (Leo, Sagittarius, Aries).

☾

Equally suitable is the period of the *descending* moon (Gemini to Sagittarius), because the tree sap is not climbing and will not run out of the cuts.

The most unfavorable time is when the moon is waxing and it is a leaf day (Cancer, Scorpio, Pisces). The tree loses too much sap and the formation of fruit is inhibited. Admittedly the fruit tree will not be destroyed, but the crop yield will go down or sometimes fail altogether. However, if the pruning is carried out precisely when the full moon is in Cancer, then there's no longer any guarantee that the plant will even survive.

GRAFTING

ONE OF THE more difficult jobs in the garden is the improvement of fruit trees through budding or grafting. Grafting, or binding a high-grade fruit-bearing or flower-bearing scion on to the stock of a common but prolific base plant, is generally done with the aim of producing a healthy and vigorous growth coupled with an increased power of resistance. It is a task that usually only very clever gardeners dare to take on. However, anyone can manage it, provided they observe the following rule:

☾

The right moment: Grafting on to fruit trees should take place when the moon is waxing, preferably close to full moon and on a fruit day (Aries, Leo, Sagittarius).

☾

The sap of the tree climbs quickly into the new scion and links it more effectively with the root system below ground. It is best to take care of this task on a fruit day. The tree will bear fruit every year. If for reasons of time you are prevented from carrying out this job during the waxing or full moon, you should choose the *ascending* moon, likewise preferably on a fruit day (Aries).

Here, too, there are different possibilities for the same task. Time constraints are not so severe as to cause one to have put the work off for a whole year if a suitable moment has been missed. Nature-lovers are not the only ones that have to take into account the weather and other surprises. If it is impossible to select the most favorable day, then at least it would be a good idea not to bring down all the negative influences at once on the plant.

An (Almost) Infallible Treatment
for Sick Plants and Trees

On July 12th, 1984, a devastating hailstorm struck the German town of Munich and its environs, causing damage running into the billions of dollars. For years afterwards there were dented cars on the streets of Munich bearing witness to the force of the tennis ball-sized hailstones. There was also long-term damage that only came to light months later: many conifers had lost their tips, which had been chopped off by the hail. Subsequently they slowly began to rot, starting at the top, until finally the trees died. In many cases the connection was not recognized, and people ascribed the dying off of the trees to what is known as "forest death" (as a consequence of the general air pollution in the Western Hemisphere)— a highly misleading expression, for the forest is not dying by itself: it should really be called "forest killing." And the solution to the puzzle? Precisely on July 12th, 1984 there was a full moon. So the weather had struck right at the most unfavorable moment; for the removal at full moon of the tip of a conifer tree or the tips of several branches of a deciduous tree can seriously damage healthy trees or even cause them to die. Sick trees are condemned to death: they rot from the tip downwards.

Exactly the same action—lopping off the tips or trimming the branches—can have the opposite effect if it is carried out on or shortly before the new moon:

℃

The right moment: All plants and trees that refuse to grow any more, or that are stunted or sickly, can in most cases be successfully treated by removing their tips when the moon is on the wane—in the fourth quarter, or best of all at new moon. The tip should be removed just above a side-branch,

*which will then push upward and adapt itself to become a
new tip.*

☾

This rule is applicable to all plants that refuse to grow properly,
including ornamental plants and blooms. Simply cut off the tips at
new moon: the results will surprise you.

Where I come from we use lengthened tree-pruners to cut off the
tips of sickly or stunted trees—almost always with success. I am certain that the many sickly trees in our forests could be helped a lot
if people would only take this simple measure.

In the case of flowers, shrubs, and fruit trees, one sometimes has
to cut away more than just the tip. With one of my own fruit trees
I ruthlessly chopped everything away just a short distance above the
grafting area. The tree put forth new shoots, and since then it has
blossomed and borne fruit every year.

As to the question of whether cutting off the tips at new moon
could stop "forest killing." I'm not sure about that, because this
would not eliminate the causes. What is certain is that the results
exceed all expectations. All sick trees that I have treated in this way
have become healthy again.

VIRGO DAYS—WORKDAYS

Virgo   when the moon is **waxing**   when the moon is **waning**
              March to September   September to March

In the garden and the countryside the zodiac sign Virgo plays a
very special role, as you may already have gathered from the directions

given so far. When it is a matter of planting and sowing, that is the best zodiac sign, but there are also one or two other tasks for which it is favorable.

Mountain foresters, for example, still know a great deal about the importance of these days. Tree cuttings can be planted without much bother during Virgo: at fairly large intervals a slit is dug with a spade; the cutting is put into it and the soil simply trodden down. If one or two saplings refuse to grow properly, then their little tips are nipped off at new moon. The trees will grow rapidly and robustly; and it is often unnecessary to fence them in as a protection against damage caused by browsing wild animals. Where I live, as far as I know, saplings are not fenced in.

Plants such as geraniums that are repotted during Virgo have the best prospects of becoming gorgeous, healthy balcony plants. Cuttings take root quickly in autumn, because then Virgo is always in the waning moon.

Cuttings can also be planted in spring when the moon is waxing. This is true above all for geraniums that are over-wintered. After their "winter sleep" the geraniums are re-potted or divided during the Virgo days, or else cuttings are simply planted from them.

Likewise a lawn sown during *Virgo* days in the *waxing moon* becomes a feast for the eyes; however, the Leo days in the waxing moon might be even more suitable for a lawn. In any case the waxing moon is important.

Town administrations could save themselves large sums of money if they would pay attention to these times when laying out town parks and lawns. The grass grows more vigorously and is much more resistant; and a second sowing often turns out to be unnecessary.

One major exception to the Virgo rules is the growth of lettuce. If it is planted in Virgo it shoots up and doesn't form a head. It "bolts," as the gardeners often say.

Sagittarius, too, is a bad sign for planting lettuce. The rules for leaf vegetables are different:

☽

Leaf vegetables (lettuce, spinach, cabbage, etc.) should be sown and planted when the moon is waning, preferably during Cancer days.

☽

Virgo days are also suitable for another job in the garden: erecting or renewing fences. However, the waning moon or new moon should be in force. Posts driven in at this time automatically stay firmly lodged. This rule applies when setting up any kind of timber posts: the waning moon fixes them firmly in place. In any case, repair work of this sort usually comes up in the autumn or early spring, when Virgo occurs in the waning moon.

Of course the moon only remains for two or three days in Virgo each month; but whatever you manage to do by way of planting work during these days will be well worth the effort. In particular, anyone who has in mind a complete reorganization of the garden would be well advised to carry out all planting and transplanting work during Virgo days when the moon is waxing. The only plants that do not absolutely need to be planted in Virgo are those that take root easily anyway—as long as one adheres to the waxing moon, or the descending moon. Set yourself priorities: during Virgo keep your aim on all the plants that are problematic, and you will come through with flying colors.

FEEDING PLANTS

IN THE PURSUIT OF LEARNING, EVERY DAY SOMETHING IS ACQUIRED.
IN THE PURSUIT OF TAO, EVERY DAY SOMETHING IS DROPPED.
LESS AND LESS IS DONE UNTIL NON-ACTION IS ACHIEVED.
WHEN NOTHING IS DONE, NOTHING IS LEFT UNDONE.
THE WORLD IS RULED BY LETTING THINGS TAKE THEIR COURSE.
IT CANNOT BE RULED BY INTERFERING.

—Lao Tsu

GENERAL RULES FOR USING FERTILIZER

All *excessive* use of fertilizers—which is nowadays the rule rather than the exception—prevents the normal formation of roots, especially in the case of fruit trees. The quantity of fertilizer should always be determined according to the need of the plant, and this is generally far less than is commonly assumed these days, particularly if one pays attention to the correct moment for putting on fertilizer.

As everywhere in the garden and field, feeling and common-sense should be the yardstick, rather than rules, dogma, and expert opinion. Good compost and dung, for instance, are still unbeaten as fertilizers, especially for fruit trees.

However, merely refraining from spreading fertilizer is only helpful in rare cases—unless you really know how to till the soil in an expert fashion. One farmer we know has not been using any fertilizer on his vegetable and cereal fields for the last ten years! And all this with very good yields of high quality crops. When asked about his method, he said: "Taking it slowly is the whole secret." Apparently he had learned his method from an old farmer. During every dry period in the vegetation phase he tills the soil in a variety of ways, using a piece of equipment that he developed himself—only as long as the soil is warm and also only going down as deeply as the warmth reaches. When the moon is waxing he only tills shallow furrows; when it is on the wane he goes deeper.

This method automatically leads in the course of time to the soil being "touched" by all 12 energy impulses. Could it be that a basic principle of the agriculture of the next millennium lies hidden here? Even so, there are of course many good reasons for a thorough discussion of the subject of fertilizer use.

An important observation in the natural world seems to have slipped completely into oblivion: during the period of the waning moon, starting after the day of full moon, the earth is able to absorb much more liquid than when the moon is waxing.

Not all that long ago I was listening one morning to a discussion on the radio between environmentalists and representatives of the farming community. The argument raged this way and that, for and against the use of fertilizer; and the importance of protecting the groundwater came up as an issue. There was no agreement in sight. I wanted to phone in and tell the participants that both sides were right, but then I decided against it.

It really is so simple: if it is spread at certain times the fertilizer works itself into the soil, can be useful for the plants and does not go into the groundwater. At other times the fertilizer stays lying on the surface, and because the materials are not taken up by the soil they pass straight into the groundwater and contaminate it.

Whenever possible, one should avoid putting down fertilizer when the moon is waxing. This just pollutes the groundwater, with all the consequences we know so well. In some areas even babies can no longer be safely given the drinking water on account of the high nitrate content.

Every farmer and gardener has discovered this in the course of his daily work: on some days spreading fertilizer has devastating effects—the turf is scorched, roots atrophy or die. On other days the fertilizer produces the desired result and there are no harmful side effects.

And so, next time you put down fertilizer pay attention to the position of the moon and observe how well the soil absorbs the substance in question when the moon is on the wane. This applies just as well to indoor and balcony plants.

℃

Whenever possible fertilizer should be put down at full moon or when the moon is waning.

℃

Often it is difficult to reconcile setting aside the full moon day as a day for putting down fertilizer with the complex work schedules of gardeners and farmers. However, keeping to this should not present a problem for many amateur gardeners—and the period of the waning moon is long enough even for larger businesses to be able to take advantage of it.

You will be surprised at the effect that comes from selecting the correct moment. You can ignore the instructions on the various preparations and gradually wean your plants from excessive dependence on fertilizers. Your successes will vindicate you.

FERTILIZING FLOWERS

The choice of zodiac sign as the moment to put down fertilizer can also play an important part. In addition to the waning moon, one should also ensure that flower fertilizing, like watering, is done on leaf days—i.e. Cancer, Scorpio, or Pisces.

For flowers that have a weak root formation, you may select a root day from time to time (Taurus, Virgo, Capricorn).

Flowers that do not seem to want to bloom any more should occasionally be given fertilizer on a flower day (Gemini, Aquarius, Libra). Not too frequently, though; otherwise it's an open invitation to aphids.

Obviously the natural, seasonal wilting of flowers should not be taken as a signal to put down fertilizer on a flower day.

Cereals, Vegetables, and Fruit

Cereals, vegetables, and fruit should not just bloom well: they should bear fruit that is full of vitality.

℃

The most suitable time for putting down fertilizer is during the fruit days (Aries, Sagittarius), here, too, when the moon is full or on the wane. Leo days are not as suitable for fertilizer because at that time soil and plants become very parched.

℃

However, you should *never use artificial fertilizer during Leo*: soil and seeds are easily scorched, particularly when the ground is dry in any case. Leo is the "fieriest" sign of the whole zodiac.

Compost Heaps—Recycling the Natural Way

Since good, fully matured compost is one of the best things produced in the garden, not just as a good fertilizer, we should discuss it in somewhat greater depth. Even twenty years ago the word "recycling" was hardly known. Perhaps it was necessary to think up an artificial word for a circular process that previously was taken for granted: whatever one receives as a gift from nature, one gives back to her so that her inner strength and wholeness is maintained.

Today the balance has shifted. We are wresting away too much from nature; not only that, we are processing, altering, and transforming her gifts to such an extent that they return to her in an indigestible and poisonous form. The bough we are sitting on is already being sawed through.

Perhaps that is why we have invented the word recycling, because our guilty consciences compel us to forget that "reuse" and "returning things to nature's round" are nothing new, but simply expressions of a necessity. Obedience to this necessity creates work, reduces yields and profits, and is "uncomfortable." Meanwhile, fortunately, a great many people have rediscovered from experience that it can also make them happy.

Making *compost* is one of the oldest forms of recycling. This chapter will perhaps not have much new to offer skilled gardening buffs, but the constantly growing problems caused by rubbish have inspired many novices in recent years to try their hand at this art. Detailed descriptions are to be found in many gardening books, so we shall confine ourselves here to one or two tips:

- The correct place for a compost heap is protected as much as possible from the wind and lying in half shadow in order to avoid drying out. It's important that there should be enough warmth for rotting to take place; a position that is too shady slows down the process of transformation.
- When you have decided on a place, the surface of the ground where the compost heap is to go should be loosened up to a depth of about four inches. Another suitable

alternative to this is a four-inch-thick bottom layer of some dry, absorbent material, such as dry grass cuttings, twigs cut up small, mulch, or straw.

❧ The base layer is then covered with loose, bulky material. The ground must not be covered with concrete or plastic or sealed in any other way. That would only lead to putrefaction and a build-up of moisture and would block the way for worms coming up into the compost heap from below.

❧ The construction of the enclosing framework of planks and the starting of the compost heap should take place when the moon is waning; the material should be stamped tight when the moon is waxing, preferably one or two days before full moon. Alternatively the compost heap could be started off when the moon is descending. If these times are adhered to, rotting takes place considerably faster; so at least one of these impulses should be kept in mind.

❧ Now it is possible to start building up the compost. Place organic material and rubbish loosely, layer by layer, one on top of the other. Suitable for compost are all decomposable materials from plant or animal rubbish that do not contain harmful substances. Branches should first be chopped up small. Diseased parts of plants do not belong in compost. Similarly, not all kitchen rubbish is suitable: the compost heap shouldn't become a rubbish dump. For instance, leftovers from cooked meals have no place on the compost heap. The remains of meals are not really kitchen rubbish and sooner or later they will attract undesirable vermin or even rats.

❧ On earth days, especially Virgo (but also Taurus and Capricorn), attention should be paid when adding biological rotting agents (such as powdered stone). Lime additives promote the formation of humus and healthy rotting.

❧ As an aid to the rotting process one can mix in half-ripe compost or garden soil between the individual layers. Repeatedly insert bulky materials, and when the moon is waxing tramp it all down several times. Grass cuttings should never be piled too high, because otherwise putrefaction will set in (two to four inches is enough). Manure is suitable for providing additional enrichment with nutrients.

❧ Dry material can be moistened a little before being piled on. A rule of thumb for building up layers:

Dry material on top of damp.

Coarse material on top of fine.

❧ Good compost may well have a pleasant smell, but even so, you shouldn't put your heap right next to your neighbor's sitting area. Your compost heap can be sheltered effectively by means of a hedge or a row of runner beans.

If you observe these rules you will be able to harvest wonderful, ripe compost, which provides the best garden soil and fertilizer.

HARVESTING, STORING, AND PRESERVING

WHAT IS THE use of all our skill at planting, sowing, and tending, if pests, molds, or putrefying bacteria reduce all our efforts to nothing? Since time immemorial, methods of storing and preserving fruits from garden, field, and forest have been employed, which allowed our forebears to survive hard winters—fermentation, salting, smoking, boiling, roasting, drying, and many more. But in addition, over and above all of these is paying attention to correct timing when harvesting and conserving.

So often measures to store and preserve food lead to variable results, although in each case the same rules of cleanliness are adhered to. The best example is this: almost every housewife has observed that now and then a jar of jam spoils after being opened for only a short time, while sometimes it can stand for weeks on the breakfast table and still taste like it did on the first day. Even without being opened, preserved fruit or homemade jams keep for varying lengths of time. Perhaps you will see the solution to this riddle when you have become acquainted with the rules for harvesting and storing.

☾

The most favorable time for harvesting, preserving, and storing is when the moon is ascending (Sagittarius to Gemini). Harvesting and storing are thus less dependent on the phase of the moon than on the sign of the zodiac through which the moon is currently passing.

The most suitable days for harvesting and storing cereals, vegetables, and potatoes are in Aries.

☾

Fruit and vegetables are juicier when the moon is *ascending*, and they stay that way if they are harvested then; thus they have the best chance of tasting good and keeping for a long time.

Preserving jams and juices is equally favorable when the moon is *ascending*. The fruit is much juicier and the aroma is much better, too. They keep longer and one can happily dispense with artificial setting agents or similar chemical additives (this applies also to preserving and bottling other foodstuffs).

Pisces days are an exception: granted they occur in the ascending moon, but anything harvested at this time should be set aside for immediate consumption. This period is not suitable for storing and preserving fruit and vegetables. There is a danger of the food going bad, and everything has a stale taste.

If for reasons of time you have to switch to another schedule, you should at least take care to steer clear of the most negative influences.

Garden and field produce harvested when the moon is *waxing* should be consumed as soon as possible, if the moon is not currently in a sign that has ascending force.

Virgo days should be avoided at all costs when harvesting, storing, and preserving. Preserved foods, for instance, can very easily start to go moldy. Cancer is not especially suitable, either; so anyone observing the ascending moon should steer clear of this sign.

Arable crops and herbs that are to be dried should always be gathered and harvested when the moon is *on the wane.*

One should only clean cellar shelves when the moon is *waning* (during an air or a fire sign). This will keep them dry and prevent mold forming.

THE SIGNS OF THE ZODIAC
IN GARDEN AND FIELD

Aries
Aries days are fruit days with ascending force.

Very favorable: ❧ sowing and planting anything that is supposed to grow fast and is intended for immediate use

❧ grafting fruit trees (when the moon is waxing)

Favorable:	❧ harvesting and storing cereals
	❧ planting and sowing fruit
	❧ cultivating cereals (when the moon is waxing)
	❧ fertilizing cereals, vegetables and fruit (must be when the moon is waning or at full moon, April to September)
	❧ pruning fruit trees and bushes (when the moon is waning)

Taurus

Taurus days are root days with ascending force.

Very favorable:	❧ sowing and planting trees, bushes, hedges, and root vegetables. Everything grows slowly and lasts well; harvest produce is especially suitable for storage.
Favorable:	❧ setting up a manure or compost heap (when the moon is waning, May to October)
	❧ combating vermin found in the soil
	❧ occasionally putting down fertilizer for flowers with poorly formed roots
	❧ preserving and storing root vegetables (e.g. potatoes, carrots, etc.)

Gemini

Gemini days are flower days and the nodal point between the ascending and descending forces.

Very favorable:	❧ planting and sowing any creeping or climbing plants

Favorable:
- planting and sowing flowers
- combating pests
- occasionally putting down fertilizer for flowers that no longer bloom properly

Cancer

Cancer days are leaf days with descending force.

Very favorable:
- setting and sowing leaf vegetables (lettuce planted when the moon is on the wane forms a good head)
- combating pests above ground

Favorable:
- mowing lawns (even better when the moon is waxing)
- watering indoor and balcony plants
- putting fertilizer around flowers

Unfavorable:
- setting and sowing plants that are to grow tall
- pruning fruit trees and bushes (when the moon is waxing, especially in spring. Cancer at full moon is particularly unfavorable)
- storing and preserving in the cellar is also unfavorable]

Leo

Leo days are fruit days with descending force.
Leo is the "fieriest" and most parching sign in the whole zodiac.

Very favorable:
- gathering herbs that strengthen the heart
- pruning fruit trees and bushes (when the

moon is waning, suitable days for winter cutting)

🐦 best day for cultivating cereals (when the moon is waxing) on wet fields

Favorable: 🐦 ssowing lawns (when the moon is waxing)

🐦 planting fruit, but nothing that requires a large amount of water (tomatoes, potatoes)

🐦 planting vegetables that are highly perishable

🐦 planting trees and bushes

🐦 grafting fruit trees (when the moon is waxing in spring)

Unfavorable: 🐦 using artificial fertilizer

Virgo

Virgo days are root days with descending force. They are the best days for almost every type of work in garden, field, and forest that is connected with setting, transplanting and new planting.

Very favorable: 🐦 all planting and sowing work. The soil lets everything open up beautifully

🐦 planting single trees that are meant to grow very tall

🐦 planting hedges and bushes that are meant to grow very fast

🐦 transplanting old trees (spring or autumn)

🐦 re-potting and new planting balcony and indoor plants

🐦 sowing lawns (when the moon is waxing)

🐦 planting cuttings (when the moon is waxing, in autumn when the moon is on the wane)

Favorable: ∾ setting up a manure or compost heap (when the moon is waning)

∾ all types of fertilizer spreading

∾ combating vermin found in the soil

∾ occasionally putting down fertilizer for flowers with poorly formed roots

∾ erecting fence posts

∾ spreading manure

Unfavorable: ∾ planting lettuce (it runs to leaf)

∾ making pickles and preserves, storing

Libra

Libra days are flower days with descending force. It is a neutral sign, and there is hardly any task in the garden that is particularly affected either favorably or unfavorably.

Favorable: ∾ sowing and planting flowers and flowering medicinal herbs

∾ occasionally putting down fertilizer for flowers that no longer bloom properly]

Scorpio

Scorpio days are leaf days with descending force.

Very favorable: ∾ sowing, planting, and also harvesting and drying every kind of medicinal herb

∾ combating slugs and snails (when the moon is waxing)

Favorable: ∾ setting and sowing leaf vegetables

- 🌙 mowing lawns
- 🌙 watering indoor and balcony plants
- 🌙 spreading fertilizer for flowers and meadows (not as good for vegetables)

Unfavorable: 🌙 pruning fruit trees and bushes (when the moon is waxing, especially in spring)
- 🌙 felling trees (danger of bark beetle)

Sagittarius

Sagittarius days are fruit days and the nodal point between ascending and descending forces.

Very favorable: 🌙 planting and sowing all fruit and all vegetables that grow tall (runner beans, hops, etc.)

Favorable: 🌙 pruning fruit trees and bushes (when the moon is waning in spring)
- 🌙 cereal cultivation, particularly maize
- 🌙 putting down fertilizer for cereals, vegetables and fruit in spring (must be when the moon is on the wane or at full moon)
- 🌙 combating pests above ground

Unfavorable: 🌙 hoeing and harrowing (weeds tend to grow in abundance afterwards)
- 🌙 planting lettuce (tends to bolt)

Capricorn

Capricorn days are root days with ascending force.

Very favorable   🌙 harrowing weeds (when the moon is waning)

Favorable:
- planting and sowing root vegetables and winter vegetables
- clearing and thinning out plants, forest edges, and hedges (when the moon is waning)
- setting up a manure or compost heap (when the moon is waning)
- combating vermin found in the soil
- occasionally putting down fertilizer for flowers with poorly formed roots
- Preserving and storing root vegetables (for instance slicing up sauerkraut, when the moon is on the wane. When the moon is waxing the fermentation process takes place too quickly)

Aquarius

Aquarius days are flower days with ascending force. However, they are unsuitable for almost all gardening tasks. One should confine oneself to what is most necessary. In garden, field and forest Aquarius is a somewhat infertile sign.

Favorable:
- hoeing and harrowing; the weeds can be left to rot
- occasionally putting down fertilizer for flowers that no longer bloom properly

Unfavorable:
- pricking out, because the transplanted seedlings will not take root and so they will die

Pisces

Pisces days are leaf days with ascending force. Everything harvested on these days should be consumed at once.

Favorable:
- planting and sowing leaf vegetables
- watering indoor and balcony plants
- mowing lawns
- fertilizing flowers
- planting potatoes when the moon is waning (especially good when Pisces falls on the *third day after full moon*)

Unfavorable:
- pruning fruit trees and bushes (when the moon is waxing, especially in spring)
- preserving and storing

F O U R

Correct Timing in Farming and Forestry

THREE THINGS ARE NEEDED IN ORDER TO DEFEAT ANY ADVERSARY:

TO BE GLAD WHEN HE IS RIGHT,

TO BE SAD WHEN HE IS WRONG,

AND NEVER TO BEHAVE FOOLISHLY TOWARD HIM.

FOUR THINGS ARE NEEDED TO SAVE THE WORLD FROM HUMANITY:

ACCEPT THE IGNORANCE OF OTHERS

AND SPARE THEM YOUR OWN.

GIVE TO THEM FROM YOUR SUBSTANCE

AND EXPECT NO PART OF THEIRS.

—Indian proverb

ALL THE RULES in the previous chapter are fully valid regardless of whether your lettuce or your fruit are grown in tiny gardens or in acre-sized fields. The principles of the lunar cycles may easily be transferred to any task in field or plantation. However, there are one or two rules of cultivation that are only of use in farming and forestry, and so a whole chapter has been devoted to them.

It is clear of course that farming has undergone enormous changes in recent decades—both voluntary and enforced, for better and for worse. Highly organized programs of work mean that a return to an observance of the lunar rhythms is not an easy matter, particularly in large-scale agricultural and livestock enterprises. But perhaps after reading the previous chapter you will have gained a deeper insight into the dynamic cycles of nature, which have not changed at all for thousands of years. Perhaps you have even found a plausible explanation for many a puzzling experience you have had with sowing, planting, harvesting, and storing.

For many "small" farmers this knowledge is very interesting and also has practical applications. Many town dwellers and customers nowadays will go a long way in search of healthy cereals, healthy meat and "milk from happy cows." If the demand continues to change in the direction of natural, healthy products, then it will be precisely such farmers that have the best chance.

Basically all gardeners, farmers, and foresters are in the same boat: they profit from the harmonious interplay of heaven and earth, of sun, wind, clouds, water, and warmth. It is not always their fault that some of the laws that prevail between heaven and earth have apparently slipped into oblivion and have led to many problems—the excessive use of fertilizers, the poisoning of the soil, the contamination of the groundwater, and the quality of the harvest, to name a few.

However, the signs that things are taking a turn for the better are on the increase: it has become clear to many people that the price of disregarding natural rhythms and cycles is much higher in the long term than the short term gains in agricultural and livestock yields. The North American Indians knew this from the outset:

ONLY WHEN THE LAST TREE HAS BEEN CLEARED,

THE LAST RIVER POISONED,

THE LAST FISH CAUGHT,

WILL YOU DISCOVER THAT YOU CANNOT EAT MONEY.

—*Native American proverb*

And it is especially in their country, which has been so severely exploited by maize-farming and other monocultures, that the march has begun toward the agriculture of the future. Large concerns have been transformed into many little ones; in the truest sense of the word environmental protection is gaining ground. Fields are again being surrounded with hedges and avenues of trees.

Perhaps it is helpful to remind ourselves once more that it was precisely the ancestors of present-day farmers and foresters, especially woodland and mountain farmers, who discovered, preserved, and passed on the knowledge of natural rhythms.

The rules presented in this book certainly cannot be applied overnight to agriculture and forestry. It will be a slow process, but one that will only get under way when the will and intention are available. Just how great the interest is, especially among farmers, has often become apparent in recent years.

Here is a suggestion: simply reserve one or several small plots, and try out all the rules of plant cultivation that are introduced in this book. Do not make any changes in your other work programs. And then just observe how these little bits of land develop.

A wealth of ideas and faith in the future created the farming methods of today; the same pioneering spirit will shape the farming and forestry of the future. If in the process a little more common sense and moderation prevail, if the lessons of the past and present are learned, then we can't go far wrong.

LUNAR CYCLES IN FARMING

CEREAL CULTIVATION

IF SOMEONE SOWING cereals manages to catch *both waxing and descending moon*, and on top of that a *fruit day* (Leo, Sagittarius), then the only thing left that could wreck his plans would be the weather.

If it is raining cats and dogs on these "best" days, no farmer will venture into the fields. Thank heaven that nature is arranged in such a way that not everything always fits neatly together.

℃

Aries and Sagittarius days are especially suitable for cultivating cereals, but so also are Leo days. However, in very dry fields there is a danger in Leo of the soil becoming parched.

Leo days are also good when the field is initially very moist.

The fruit day Aries is the best time for storing cereals.

℃

"LOT" DAYS

Perhaps you have already wondered why a particular variety of cereal turns out particularly well in some years and particularly badly in others. Of course wind and weather, seed quality and soil characteristics play a part. And yet sometimes one farmer will succeed in bringing in a good harvest, while his neighbor, working under the same conditions, only achieves a miserable yield.

With your knowledge of the rules concerning the correct times for sowing, fertilizing, and harvesting, it is possibly already clear to you that one main reason for the differing yields is to be found here.

In this connection you should be made aware of an odd rule that formerly almost every farmer knew, and which according to our own personal experiments is still entirely valid. It concerns two days in the year: July 8th and July 20th.

℃

*The correct moment: Anyone wishing to find out which type
of cereal will produce the best harvest in the following year
should sow a few grains of each cereal variety in the ground.
The seeds that have sprouted the best on July 20th will also
flourish the best in the coming year.*

℃

Try this rule out in a test bed. The results will speak for themselves. These days belong to the so-called "lot days." The origin of
their names lies in the fact that formerly these days were seen as a
sort of "lot" that could be "drawn." Based on this "lot," i.e., what
happened on these days, people predicted future events, principally connected with the way the weather would develop.

*Apart from that, I do not wish to deal with the lot days in this book,
although I know that even today many farmers observe the lot days, especially the weather rules connected with them, and many of these are still perfectly valid today. I have often been able to observe this.*

*However the worldwide changes in climate have caused what was for-
merly an extremely important and useful instrument to go somewhat out of
control. For this reason we shall not go further into the matter here.*

MILK PROCESSING

Almost every form of milk processing is at its most successful on *fat*
days, i.e., Gemini, Libra, and Aquarius. Also suitable are the warmth
days of Aries, Leo, and Sagittarius. Neutral days are Taurus, Virgo,
and Capricorn. Unsuitable days are Cancer, Scorpio, and Pisces; on
such days one can churn and churn and no butter will come.

When making cheese the phase of the moon plays an important part; but it all depends *what sort* of cheese is to be produced. If it is to mature slowly then the waning moon is more suitable; for slow-maturing cheeses the waxing moon is more favorable. In general Virgo is not a favorable sign for cheese production; the fruit days are more suitable.

PESTS AND WEEDS

All the advice given in the previous chapter for combating weeds and pests is also applicable in the farming industry. We shall therefore only point out here that enormous quantities of weed killers and pesticides could be saved if only this advice were heeded.

PUTTING DOWN FERTILIZER

As we have already mentioned, the earth is able to absorb more liquid when the moon is on the wane than when it is waxing. Recently there has been much discussion in the media because ministries of agriculture all over the world are having to budget colossal sums for the protection of water resources as a result of the pollution of groundwater and rivers with excess fertilizer—phosphates and nitrates from agriculture and waste water. It is certain that a large part of this money could be saved if attention were paid to lunar cycles when using fertilizers.

The fact that the absorbency of the earth varies can also be established indirectly. Have you ever noticed that flooding is much more common when the moon is waxing? At this time the earth is unable to absorb so much water. On the other hand steep mountain slopes are much more liable to landslides when the moon is waning, because the earth is wet and heavy and saturated—particularly if there are no healthy trees firmly anchored in the soil, or if the mountain forest is sick. This connection is very important for modern agriculture and forestry and for the protection of water resources, and it urgently requires renewed attention.

Practically every farmer knows this: on some days putting down fertilizer has disastrous effects, while on other days the desired result is achieved. If one has learned the rules, the situation is no longer so puzzling.

☾

Wherever possible, fertilizer or manure should be spread when the moon is waning. With cereals, vegetables, and fruit, ideally on fruit days (Aries, Leo, Sagittarius), otherwise during Virgo or on another earth day (Taurus, Capricorn).

Liquid manure should be spread if possible when the moon is full. Alternatively, at least when the moon is on the wane. Then the groundwater will remain unharmed.

Never spread artificial manure during Leo! The plants will be scorched because Leo has a severely desiccating effect.

When starting a dung heap the waning moon is also a great help.

☾

One could argue that the stench would cause a great nuisance if every farmer were to spread liquid manure at the same time. And yet it is surely preferable to put up with the "stink" for three days rather than poisoning the groundwater.

When using fertilizer let your judgment be guided by feeling and common sense. Good compost and manure are still unsurpassed as fertilizers, especially for fruit trees.

HARVESTING AND STORING CEREALS

Good results can be obtained if the farmer is able to harvest and store his cereal crops during the *ascending* moon, or, alternatively, when the moon is *on the wane*, especially during *Aries* or on another *fruit day*. The cereal will then be much longer lasting and less susceptible to beetles and mold. One could thus avoid spending enormous sums on pesticides.

All water days are *unsuitable*: storing away should be avoided at that time.

PATHS AND WATERCOURSE MANAGEMENT

Many architects and builders have learned through experience that paving stones laid out of doors sometimes become wobbly after a short time and that verandas or paths covered with gravel become uneven, despite all their care and expertise. On another occasion the path stays as firm as if it were set in concrete. Here, too, the timing of the work is of decisive importance for a successful outcome.

As for the rules of watercourse management observe the variable effect of flood water in the bed of a stream: when the stream is in spate during the waxing moon the water leaves behind a lot of gravel in the bed of the stream, i.e. the stream overflows its banks more often; when the moon is waning the stream washes and carries the gravel away.

    ∿ **Country tracks** should also be laid or filled with gravel when the moon is *on the wane*. The *Capricorn days* are especially suitable for this. If the work is done when the moon is waxing, the surface remains loose, subsides, or becomes rutted. The very first rain will wash the new gravel away.

- **Paving stones** in the garden or on paths should also be laid when the moon is *waning*. If they are laid out when the moon is waxing they eventually become wobbly. This is especially important with the paving around entrance gates, because the immense weight of vehicles rapidly dislodges the paving stones or often even breaks them.

- **Excavating springs or searching for water** should be undertaken in the star sign *Pisces* when the moon is waxing (if possible in the second quarter, close to full moon. *Never* work on a spring when the moon is on the wane or descending: the water will disappear and find another path for itself.

- **Building up the banks of streams and rivers** (embedding rocks and timber) should be done during a *water sign* (Cancer, Scorpio, Pisces) when the moon is *waxing*.

   If this is carried out when the moon is waning the built-up bank will be undermined and washed away and the river will overflow.

- **Work on drainage and sewage and repairing water pipes** is likewise most successful when the moon is *waxing* during a *water sign*.

FENCES

The most suitable time for erecting or renewing fences is when the moon is *on the wane or new*. Posts driven into the ground at this time automatically remain firm, particularly during the earth days (Virgo). Nails in wood stay firmly in place.

This rule applies when erecting posts of all sorts: the waning moon makes them firm. The day of the new moon is the most favorable for such tasks. In autumn the equally favorable Virgo days are always in the waning moon (September to February).

Alternatively the *descending* moon is also suitable; however, the closer to full moon the less favorable it is.

SETTING UP HAYSTACKS

The best time to set up a haystack is when the moon is *on the wane.* The hay remains well ventilated and dry; it does not rot and the danger of spontaneous combustion is much less.

If the moon is waxing the hay easily goes gray and moldy.

THE CARE OF ANIMAL DWELLINGS

Every farmer and farmer's spouse knows that the thorough maintenance of stables, cowsheds, and pigsties can be a tedious and time-consuming task. However, those who observe the following advice will be able to save themselves a great deal of drudgery. Of course we are not talking here about day-to-day care of animal dwellings: this has to take place regardless of the current star sign.

℃

Watch out for the waning moon (or alternatively the ascending moon) and an air sign (Gemini, Libra, Aquarius).
Persistent dirt can be removed particularly easily during water signs (Cancer, Scorpio, Pisces).

℃

The animals' quarters will remain cleaner longer, will remain protected against vermin and mold, and will dry quicker. Mold on the walls can be washed off more easily when the moon is waning (ideally using water with a little vinegar and a scrubbing brush).

The bedding straw for animals, too, should be brought in during the time of the *waning* moon. Alternatively, if time is short, one should favor the ascending moon. Incidentally a good underlay is still straw or dry beech foliage.

Any painting of the walls should be done when the moon is *waning*. This task is particularly successful on an *air* day (Gemini, Libra, Aquarius).

DRIVING THE CATTLE OUT TO PASTURE

A decisive factor in the behavior of animals in pasture is the day that they are driven out for the first time in the year. If one chooses the descending moon (especially during the Libra days), then the animals are happy to stay out in the meadows and do not try to go home before they have eaten their fill. At the same time, however, the day chosen should be a Monday, Wednesday, Friday, or Saturday.

One should *never* drive the cattle out to pasture for the first time on a *Tuesday* or a *Thursday*! This rule is still observed today in the Alps, particularly at the time of the annual drive up to and down from the alpine pastures. These two days are also unsuitable for moving cattle to other places or bringing them home from market. They are not so generous with their milk and often will not conceive subsequently.

One should also avoid *Leo* and *Cancer* days. Driving cattle out on these days makes them wild, and then they are difficult to control. During Cancer they are forever returning to the cowshed door, especially cattle grazing on alpine pastures.

In autumn cattle should be put out to pasture for the last time when the moon is *waxing*.

CALVING

When cows are in calf around about the new year, the calves are born around October. These will be the healthiest calves, and almost always the vet will be able to stay home at the time of birth. It is important to take care that the cows do not calve again too soon after that.

HEALTHY CHICKENS — HEALTHY HENS

For hens, too, there are equivalent rules: the best chickens are produced if the hens' eggs are incubated, whether by the hens themselves or in an incubator, so that the chickens hatch at full moon. The incubation period is always the same, so even in large-scale businesses it is perfectly possible to work out and stick to this rhythm.

MOVING INTO NEW QUARTERS

The period of the *ascending* moon is the most suitable time for moving into a new shed. The animals are then happier to remain inside; they do not get so restless and are not always trying to get out. Here, too, it is appropriate additionally to pay attention to the day of the week: newly bought or sold animals should never be moved from one shed to another on a Tuesday, Thursday, or Sunday. Even moving a stall-box is unfavorable on these days.

WEANING CALVES

Unfortunately, allowing calves to be suckled by the cow has gone out of fashion nowadays. Perhaps one reason for this is that the art of timing has been forgotten. It is just the same as it is with humans: for a time people believed that industrially manufactured baby food was the answer to all our problems. Now the realization is beginning to prevail that even contaminated mother's milk is still better than milk in bottles.

Start weaning calves shortly before full moon, and let them drink milk for the last time at full moon itself.

However, full moon in Leo, Cancer, or Virgo is an unfavorable time. In Leo you will have yelling animals; in Cancer they will always be coming back for more; in Virgo they often get aggressive later, and their restless behavior and brawls with other cows make them a danger for the whole herd, especially in the mountains.

RULES OF FORESTRY

WOOD IS A wonderful substance. For thousands of years it has given humanity warmth and tools, protection, and beauty through the work of the great carvers. To protect and preserve the forests of the earth, the source of all this wealth, is one of the most important tasks of our time. Fortunately there are grounds for optimism, despite the dying off of our forests through pollution, and clearance of the rain forest: countries such as Sweden, where not a single tree is cut down without a new one being planted; worldwide reforestation and the efforts of the environmentalists, who are gradually making their views felt. There is an immense contribution that could be made by the rediscovery and application of the ancient rules of forest maintenance and tree-felling to the enterprise of "saving our forests."

Wood is a substance that is full of life. Even after it has been cut down the wood "lives on": it goes on "working," to use the language of timber experts. Depending on the type of wood, the season and—as we shall see—the moment when the tree was felled, the wood will dry rapidly or slowly, stay soft or become hard, stay heavy or become light, develop cracks or remain unaltered, warp or stay flat, fall prey to rot and woodworm, or remain protected from pests and decay.

Basically, just as with all the other rules, there are no good and bad days for felling timber. The decisive factor is the *purpose* of the wood in question. It makes a big difference whether wood is intended for floors, barrels, bridges, roof trusses, musical instruments, or carving. Of course the type of wood also has to be taken into consideration, as well as its age and pattern of growth.

Trees grow either *straight* up, *spiraling to the right* or *spiraling to the left* (as can be seen from the bark). The difference is not difficult to recognize: a rightward spiraling tree screws upward like a corkscrew

LEFT SPIRALING TREE   RIGHT SPIRALING TREE

held upright. This "direction of rotation" must also be taken into account when using a particular piece of wood.

Roof shingles, for example, should either be straight-grained or slightly spiraling to the left. In wet weather the wood stretches; in sunshine, on the other hand, it twists very slightly, allowing drying air under the shingle.

With wooden *gutters*, which are sometimes still used, the converse is true: the grain of the wood should run straight or spiral slightly to the right, because right-spiraling wood "stays put" after it has been felled—that is to say, the rotation does not continue. Left-spiraling wood will cause the gutter to twist little by little and the water will run out.

The strange thing is that left-spiraling wood "works" more than right-spiraling or straight-grained wood. Furthermore lightning only strikes trees that spiral to the left—a useful piece of information if you are caught in a thunderstorm in the forest. You should only stand under a straight or rightwards-spiraling tree.

Even today in Tyrol and many other countries the correct felling times are still observed. You will get a knowing wink from many timber merchants and be led to a particular stack of timber if you insist on wood that has been cut at the correct time. Timber firms in many parts of the world, for example Brazil and the South Seas, conclude contracts in which the wood-cutters must only sell timber that has been felled at particular times.

Of course many firms no longer pay any attention to the favorable moment, either for organizational reasons, because insufficient importance is accorded to the work, or else because the knowledge is simply no longer available. On top of that, attention to correct timing appears at first sight complicated and costly, but this is not so. The work has to be done in any case. Anyone who looks out for wood that has been cut at the right time will find his labor rewarded many times over.

In the course of recent years I have got to know several people who had never previously heard anything about the correct timing for cutting wood, but who were prepared to put this ancient knowledge to the test. They were all surprised at the result—and how unfailingly these influences still hold good today.

However, this can have consequences for industry: its products—furniture, bridges, buildings, tools, timber, and many other things—would become much more durable, and render superfluous all expenditure on wood preservatives. This makes these things seem less interesting in a "throwaway" society. But it must be explicitly stressed that people who are endowed with reason and are at one with nature noticed this long ago: such a society cannot survive in the long run. Of course everyone is happy to enjoy the advantages of science, technology, and progress without thinking too much about the disadvantages. But if the possibility exists of solving the problem of waste, if the destruction of forests can be slowed down, if we can release fewer poisons into our surroundings, then everyone should know about such possibilities and be able to take advantage of them. Perhaps in the beginning a bench or a cupboard made from wood cut at the correct time would still be a little more expensive because only small businesses can afford to pay closer attention to timing, or simply because the demand exceeds the supply.

Perhaps in the future architects, joiners, carpenters, and interior decorators will unite together and commit themselves to using wood cut according to the old rules because they have recognized that environmental compatibility, quality, and durability are becoming the most important factors for more and more people when deciding to buy.

In times like today, when "ecological" house-building is gradually coming to the fore, sufficient customers could be found who would know how to appreciate such things. Anyone who commissions the building of such a house would be at pains to build in the most environmentally friendly manner. If his roof truss warps into curves after a few years or splits the wood, then even with the best will in the world he can be driven to despair. One can also often observe how natural wood and natural materials, left untreated for the best of reasons, perhaps on the facade of a house, after some years nonetheless have to be treated at considerable expense with waterproofing material for instance. The good intention was there, but watching wood getting wetter and wetter and threatening to rot makes many a builder throw up his hands. All problems of this sort could be avoided if one used wood that had been cut in accordance with the position of the moon. (Prospective builders are urged to refer once more to the short section on *paths and watercourse management*: all the advice given there applies likewise to laying paths, driveways, and paving stones, whether building a new house or simply renovating it, whether in the country or in the town.)

To anyone asking the perfectly legitimate question as to how one is to find wood nowadays that has been cut at the correct time, we can only suggest making use of the telephone services. Take a look in the Yellow Pages and call some timber merchants. Ask if you can be told the time when the wood was cut. Get an association of timber merchants to send you their list of members. Stick to your guns and don't let yourself be put off. The customer is king!

Anyone who keeps his eyes open as he travels through life will find in many places, in the Alps, for instance, and particularly in historic "museum" villages, living testimony to the validity of the rules for cutting wood at the correct time. Thus it is simply unthinkable that our forebears could have built farmhouses, mountain huts, and bridges that have withstood all kinds of weather for centuries right up to the present, which even had *fireplaces* made of wood, if they had not been in possession of this knowledge. Foresters are able to resort to their own experience any time they might doubt the validity of these rules. They know for example that damage to forests after storms has extremely variable effects on timber quality. The wood from uprooted trees is unusable in any case for building and furniture timber, but its quality as fuel and for other purposes and its susceptibility to pests is different in every case. Forest damage during Scorpio, for instance, has a catastrophic effect: the bark beetle sets upon the wood like a mouse upon cheese, after which it reproduces and then starts attacking healthy trees. This is something foresters learn to their cost, when they thin out and clear a wood during Scorpio of all times, because they do not know the correct days for this task.

Perhaps on the shelves of the U.S. Department of Forestry library there is an old book containing forestry regulations from previous centuries which speak in clear terms and give precise directions concerning the times to cut wood, taking into consideration the lunar cycles, and with the threat of "condign punishment" for disregarding them. There is many a retired forester who can probably remember the tales that his own grandfather told about how meticulously forestry workers observed the most favorable times for the various types of wood and drew up highly refined yearly plans for cutting timber. This is necessary because the best times in each case always vary slightly from one year to the next, and there are even some dates that only occur every two years or so. Timber preservatives were unknown, because the choice of the correct moment in any given case achieved the desired effects for the particular quality of wood.

The rules on the following pages will be of great interest to foresters not just in relation to times for cutting wood and wood quality. The general dying off of our forests through pollution and the hosts of sick trees in our woods are among their most pressing problems. Which is why we should like to remind you of a rule given in Chapter 3: the great hailstorm of July 12, 1984 broke off the tips of many conifers in Munich and the surrounding region. Subsequently the trees slowly began to rot, starting at the top, and finally the trees died. The relevant rule is so important that it is repeated here:

℃

All trees that will not grow any more, or that are stunted or sickly, can in most cases be successfully treated by removing their tips, or, in the case of deciduous trees, the tips of several branches in the crown of the tree, when the moon is on the wane—in the fourth quarter, or best of all at new moon.

In every case the tip should be removed just above a side-branch, which will adapt itself to become a new tip as it grows upwards.

℃

When the hailstorm broke off the tips on July 12th, at full moon, nature brought about exactly the opposite effect. The loss of the tips on this date means almost certain death for the tree: it will rot from the tip downward. Foresters should be urged to try an experiment and apply this method on a few trees. Cutting off the tips of trees isn't going to block off any factory chimneys or clean up any exhaust emissions, but it's still worth a try.

Now for wood-cutting itself: on the following pages you will also be acquainted with many special rhythms: *rules and special dates that are generally independent of the position of the moon.* Their only justification is the result that their application brings about—so just go ahead and put them into action.

The Correct Time for Cutting Wood

Almost everyone that has anything to do with cutting and processing timber knows that in general *winter* is the best time for obtaining wood. The sap has gone down, and the timber will warp less after it has been felled. However, in addition to that, there are a large number of special dates that have a clearly discernible bearing on the characteristics of wood.

The following comprehensive set of rules comes down to us from decades ago; the text you are about to look at dates back to 1912. All the rules stated in this old document are as valid as ever. They give exact directions concerning the characteristics to be obtained in each particular case.

INDICATIONS FOR WOOD-CUTTING AND WASTING DAYS

By Ludwig Weinhold
Recorded by Michael Ober, master cartwright in St Johann, Tyrol, copied by Josef
Schmutzer, December 25, 1912

1. Wasting days are April 3, July 30, and St. Achatius day, even better when these fall during the waning moon or on a Lady Saint Day. These days are also good for casting bullets and shot.
2. For timber to remain firm and tight-fitting it is good to cut it in the first eight days after new moon in December, on a day with a weak sign. For straight-wood or making-wood, beech etc. to remain tight fitting and firm, it should be new moon in Scorpio.
3. So that the wood does not rot it should be cut in the last two days of March with the waning moon in Pisces.
4. So that the wood does not burn, there is only one day when it should be cut: March 1st, preferably after sunset.
5. So that the wood does not shrink it should be cut on the third day of autumn. At the start of autumn on September 24, when the moon is three days old and on a Lady Day when it is a Cancer day.
6. Working on firewood so that it grows back well should be done in October during the first quarter of the waxing moon.
7. Timber for sawing should be cut down when the moon is waxing in Pisces; then boards and timber will not be worm-ridden.
8. Timber for bridges and arches should be cut down when the moon is waning in Pisces or Cancer.
9. So that the wood becomes light it should be cut down with the moon in Scorpio and in August. If it is cut down in Taurus, i.e. when the August moon has been waning for one day, then it will remain heavy.
10. So that the wood does not develop cracks or open up it should be cut before new moon in November.
11. So that the wood does not split, it should be cut on June 24 between 11 and 12 o'clock.
12. Straight-wood or making-wood should be cut down on February 26 when the moon is on the wane—better still on a Cancer day.

These indications have all been proven and tested.

Of course this set of rules requires a "translation" if it is to be comprehensible to everyone today. There now follows the interpretation, as well as many additional tips, arranged according to the quality or wood desired or the intention being pursued on a specific date.

❦

Bear in mind though, that all these rules are as valid as ever and will yield the desired and expected results under one provision: The trees and boards must be left and stacked to dry naturally by themselves. That process takes in general about a year until the residual humidity stops at about 20 percent. Only then it is okay to dry the wood a little further in special ovens down to around 10 percent, if one wishes to use the wood inside the house for furniture and so forth. This is not necessary if the wood is used for wooden houses, "cold roofs," or any other outside use.

❦

"WASTING DAYS"—GRUBBING AND CLEARING

Every commercial forest needs maintenance. Anyone who wishes to clear and clean up a wood or forest border, or who wishes to deforest and replant, should look out for "Wasting Days" (grubbing days), i.e., according to the rules, *April 3, July 30, and St. Achatius day (June 22).* The result of the work will be even better if these days fall during the waning moon or on a "Lady day." Trees and bushes cut down at this time will not grow back.

"Lady days" are holidays devoted to the Virgin Mary, such as the feasts of Assumption or Purification. These days can be found in any farmer's calendar (e.g. August 15 and September 8).

Alternative days for grubbing and clearing are the *last three days in February* if they fall in the waning moon. Wood cut at this time will not grow back; even the roots will rot.

WOOD FOR TOOLS AND FURNITURE

The German dialect word rendered here as "tight-fitting" originally meant "as if glued": the wood stays firm, does not warp or get dry and fall apart, it maintains its volume—an important feature for instance of skirting boards and edging strips. Wood that is cut in *the first eight days after the December new moon in Aquarius or Pisces* acquires this quality.

The German dialect words given as "straight-wood" and "making-wood" are no longer in current use. "Straight-wood" refers to wood that is used to make tools and implements (broom handles, axe hafts, etc.); it has to be light and easy to handle. "Making-wood" is wood from which things are made—furniture, cabinets, cupboards, and the like.

Wood cut when the *new moon* falls in *Scorpio* (usually in November) has the desired characteristics. However, it should have its *bark removed immediately*: for bark beetles, wood that has been cut in Scorpio or uprooted before a storm is a signal to attack. They then reproduce magnificently and even attack healthy trees.

Rule number twelve gives an equally good alternative date: February 26, *provided it falls during the waning moon* (which is not always the case), and especially if the moon is in the sign of *Cancer* at the same time (as happened for instance in 1989).

NON-ROTTING, HARD WOOD

Non-rotting wood must be cut during the last two days in March with the moon on the wane in Pisces. These days do not come round every year. So people used to look out especially for them or else cut the wood on alternative days:

These days are: *New Year's Day, January 7, January 25, and from January 31 to February 2.* Timber that is cut down on these six days will not rot or get woodworm.

Furthermore, wood that is cut at *New Year* or *between January 31 and February 2* will become very hard as it ages.

It could well be that the foundations of the magnificent "floating" buildings of Venice consist of such timber. If they had not been felled on the correct day, the splendid city would probably have sunk into the water once and for all by now. Restoring the foundations with wood of this sort would be the ideal solution, for its durability can be clearly seen from the age of the present timber. Any other solution (concrete, steel, etc.) is unsuitable in the long run. This is also the right kind of wood for landing jetties and tall buildings on pile foundations.

Alternative days are *warm summer days when the moon is waxing*: such wood is suitable for pile foundations in water, mooring piers for ships, and bathing platforms. Its sap content is then at its maximum and it should be incorporated into the structure immediately.

NON-INFLAMMABLE WOOD

Anyone who has visited a "museum village" (such as Kramsach in Tyrol), with its up to 700 centuries old buildings, barns, equipment, and tools, will have certainly also seen benches next to stoves, wooden pot holders, bread paddles, and wooden fireplaces. What is strange is that hardly anyone asks why the semicircular pot holders used for lifting red-hot pots and pans from the stove lasted for so long—for centuries even—without burning. Or why wood exposed directly to fire did not burn (e.g. wooden fireplaces, and the wooden tools used to scrape the sides of lime kilns). Admittedly it was blackened, but it neither burned nor glowed. Perhaps you, too, have come across a box of matches that absolutely refuse to burn. The solution to the puzzle is this: there are specific times whose impulses ensure that wood is non-inflammable.

☾

Wood that is cut on March 1, especially after sunset, is fire-resistant—regardless of the position of the moon and the sign through which it is currently passing.

☾

A strange and yet valid rule: whoever tries it out will find it confirmed. Many implements, farmyard buildings, barns, log cabins, and mountain huts were built out of such timber in order to make them fireproof.

My parents' house, which was completely gutted by fire in 1980, was made of wood like that. The metal of some agricultural implements inside was subsequently found to be partially melted, so great was the heat. The building itself remained standing: the wood was only charred on the outside. When it was due to be leveled with a tractor, the timber would not give way. In the end the house had to be sawn up beam by beam. We then saw that only a few inches of the outermost layer of the wood was charred; the interior had remained completely intact. Part of the timber was later reused in the construction of two new buildings.

NON-SHRINKING WOOD

In many spheres of use it is important that the wood does not shrink: in other words: that the volume does not decrease. Such wood is best cut on *St. Thomas day (December 21) between 11 and 12 o'clock.* This day is the best wood-cutting day of all. After this time timber should, with certain exceptions, only be cut down in winter when the moon is waning. Other periods suitable for cutting non-shrinking wood are: *February evenings after sunset when the moon is on the wane, September 27, every month during the three days after new moon, Lady saints' days* (among others, August 15 and September 8) when these fall on *Cancer* days. Also wood that is cut at *new moon in the sign of Libra* will not shrink and can be used immediately. Also, timber that is felled in February after sunset will become rock-hard as it ages.

FIREWOOD

Nonetheless, good *combustibility* is of course often a desirable quality in wood. Furthermore when obtaining firewood one does not want to clear the entire forest, so it is advantageous that everything should grow back well afterwards.

The rule states that the best time for cutting firewood is the *first quarter of the waxing moon in October,* that is to say the first seven days after the October new moon.

In general, however, firewood should be cut *after the winter solstice when the moon is on the wane.* But the treetop should not be removed straight away, and in hilly conditions you should leave the timber pointing downhill for some time, so that the last of the sap can be drawn to the top.

TIMBER FOR PLANKS, SAWING, AND BUILDING

The most suitable time for timber for planks and sawing is the *waxing phase of the moon in Pisces*, because the wood will not then be attacked by pests. The star sign Pisces only appears in the waxing moon from September to March.

TIMBER FOR BRIDGES AND BOATS

Have you ever crossed a wooden bridge on a rainy day? It's as well to hold tight to the railing, they are so slimy and slippery sometimes. And raft journeys can turn into nonstop sliding games if the timber for the raft was cut on the "wrong" day. On the other hand there are old wooden bridges over mountain streams in the Alps that are safe underfoot, do not rot, and seem to have been built to last forever, without any treatment with wood preservatives.

The fact that nowadays Alpine clubs and tourist organizations obviously no longer pay any heed to such influences when building bridges is something that every mountain hiker has been forced to discover. There would be no need for so many tourists to be fetched back with sprained limbs by the mountain rescue service if more attention were paid to correct timing when cutting wood.

Timber for bridges, boats, and rafts should be cut when the moon is *on the wane* in a *water sign* (Pisces or Cancer). It will not rot and will be safe under foot.

This rule also used to be observed in the choice of wood for washbasins, which have to endure constant wetting without becoming slippery.

Although Scorpio is likewise a water sign, it is nonetheless not so suitable, because the wood at that time becomes too light for this purpose and is also susceptible to attack by pests.

TIMBER FOR FLOORS AND TOOLS

Broom handles and other wood for tools should be supple and firm to hold, not easily breakable, flexible, and above all light. The best time for such wood is during the *Scorpio days in August*, which almost always come before the full moon.

If the wood is to have the above characteristics but remain heavy (for instance for wooden floors that will take a lot of strain), then one should choose *the first day after full moon* that occurs in the sign of *Taurus* (which does not happen every year).

NON-SPLITTING WOOD

Timber that must not split—for instance for furniture and carving—is best felled in the *days prior to the new moon in November*.

Equally acceptable alternatives are *March 25, June 29, and December 31.* Wood that is cut down on these three days does not break or split. Here, too, the top of the tree should point down the valley, or on level ground it should be left on the tree a little longer, so that residual sap can be drawn to the top.

Wood that is to be used quickly, for instance when rebuilding after a fire, must under no circumstances split later. The best felling time is *June 24 between 11 and 12 midday* (between 12 and 1 P.M. in the summertime). That used to be a special day. Timber workers would turn out in swarms and for a whole hour would saw for all they were worth.

The *best bridge timber* is obtained when the new moon coincides with Cancer. This rule is as valid today as it ever was.

CHRISTMAS TREES

Finally a tip for the "season of peace": **fir trees**, if they are cut down *three days before the eleventh full moon* of the year (generally in November, but sometimes in December), retain their needles for a very long time. Formerly these trees received a "moon stamp" from the forester and were somewhat more expensive than other Christmas trees. **Spruce trees** don't shed their needles then either, but should be stored in a cool place until Christmas. However, they still lose their needles earlier than firs.

A relative of mine has owned a Christmas tree like that for more than thirty years, and it still has its needles. I myself still have the first Advent wreath I made after

moving to Munich in 1969. If I pluck off a few needles, they smell sweet even today.

It would be a good idea to gather shoots for Advent garlands three days before the eleventh or twelfth full moon, because in that way beautifully laid out Advent tables won't always get covered with needles. Of course, knowledge of this rule should not be seen as entitling you to go marching into the forest and "poach" your Christmas tree there.

Naturally one cannot always get a Christmas tree that was cut exactly three days before the eleventh full moon. And so here's another tip: Christmas trees and garlands also last longer and do not lose their needles so quickly if in general one watches out for the waxing moon or the days before full moon.

Garlands of dried flowers (made from flowers that are suitable for drying) also last longer if they are picked when the moon is waxing.

FIVE

The Moon as a "Helper" in the Home and Everyday Life

SOFT CONQUERS HARD,

WEAK CONQUERS STRONG.

THE FLEXIBLE IS ALWAYS SUPERIOR TO THE IMMOVABLE.

THIS IS THE PRINCIPLE OF CONTROLLING THINGS

BY BRINGING ONESELF INTO TUNE WITH THEM,

THE PRINCIPLE OF MASTERY THROUGH HARMONY.

—Lao Tsu

THE FACT THAT the lunar cycles have slipped into oblivion in the household and in city life is hardly surprising. The wind that has been blowing for decades from the "land of limitless possibilities" bears a very special message: freedom and self-realization are basic rights that take priority over our obligations toward ourselves, our neighbors, and nature.

Western civilized man has gradually become convinced that electricity comes out of the socket, that a caustic cleansing fluid vanishes into thin air when it reaches the waste-pipe, and that the whole of life comes to him out of the television. And above all: that he has a right to rapid results, whether from cleansing, medical, or any other preparations.

Naturally in the course of time many constraints arise from this "right": two-income families are compelled to do their housework in odd moments here and there, using "fast-working" preparations and equipment. Assisted by advertising and psychology, work in the house has degenerated into a necessary evil; every promise of work made easier was joyfully received without any concern for such effects as massively increasing power consumption (of which a high percentage is the responsibility not of industry but of private households), or environmental pollution. One could almost devise a mathematical formula: the more expensive and rapidly effective, the more poisonous for mankind and the environment. The pride and satisfaction that could be derived from a well conducted household in harmony with the rhythms of nature were no longer fashionable.

Fortunately the awareness is increasing now that things cannot go on like this. The effects of such shortsightedness are catching up on us and have aroused a determination in many people to take a closer look at the "wipe-away" society, and then to make their contribution to a return to means and methods that are more easygoing on nature. However, some of them are close to despair because in many cases in the household it is only the aggressive and poisonous agents that seem to work. For such people being guided by the lunar cycles can come as something of a revelation.

Doing the housework in harmony with the rhythms of the moon is easier, more enjoyable, and reduces the already high level of stress that many people toil under. There are many tips for the daily household chores in the preceding chapters (healthy diet, cooking, herbal knowledge, home improvement, etc.), but there are many things still to be said, and some things that are worth repeating.

Especially in the household one can often very rapidly observe and check the validity of the rules.

℃

Almost all housework—which is often connected with cleaning, removing, and "flushing out"—is dealt with much

more successfully and effortlessly when the moon is on the
wane.

☾

Of course it isn't possible to postpone all work in the house to
the waning phases of the moon, and simply to twiddle one's thumbs
while the moon is waxing; however, if you can manage gradually to
move a part of the workload to this period you will be astonished
at the effects arising from even minor postponements.

Let your own experience speak for itself. There are times when
any kind of housework comes easily; at other times it simply never
ends. In practice one often notices, without being able to give a
reason for it, that things such as furniture, floors, laundry, and windows get clean more quickly and easily than on other days.
Sometimes everything goes really smoothly; sometimes anything
that can go wrong does.

This is particularly true of the laundry; only on the assumption,
however, that you do not go about it with excessively caustic substances and exaggerated quantities of chemicals, and that you do
not regularly use excessive amounts of detergent. Otherwise it may
happen that you will be unable to reproduce the observations that
follow. The effect of the lunar cycles is so subtle that it may not
seem plausible to make it directly responsible for such effects. And
yet these forces do exist and can be of great use in the long run.
When you have actually tried out this rhythm you will be able to
bring a lot of pleasure and energy to this time-consuming work.

Problem stains, for example, can be removed much more quickly when the moon is waning than when it is waxing—provided that
from the outset you pay no attention to the quantities suggested by
the detergent manufacturers and dispense with any caustic agents.
The cleaning will be even more successful if one looks out for a
water day (Pisces, Cancer, Scorpio). In addition, the environment

will be spared, since waste water is broken down more easily when the moon is waning.

> When the moon is on the wane, which is when I do most of my laundry, I myself only use a quarter of the prescribed quantity of detergent. I don't have any problems with my washing machine getting furred up either. If I find any calcium deposit in the filter I simply add a little vinegar to the water. I really think that in this way I can make my personal daily contribution to environmental protection.

Try out a simple test. When the moon is waning place a very dirty piece of clothing in a full wash basin and add some detergent or soft soap. Then when the moon is waxing do the same thing under the same conditions, and compare what happens. The result will astonish you: when the moon is waxing the water will stay nice and soapy and the laundry nice and dirty. When the moon is on the wane the dirt will come off; just by looking at the suds one can see where it has all gone. Perhaps you have also noticed that sometimes everything smells especially fresh and light, even though the laundry procedure and the quantity of detergent used were the same.

Whether a task goes smoothly or badly, whether the room or the laundry is cleaned satisfactorily, depends on the moment when the work is done. The rule of thumb with household chores is: *When the moon is waning everything is easier.*

There now follows in no particular order a sequence of special tips about household chores. If a particular star sign is mentioned in connection with a suggestion, that should not be taken to mean that this task is only worth doing on those days, but that it will be *especially successful* at that time.

DOING LAUNDRY, POLISHING, AND CLEANING

LAUNDRY DAY

Especially in families with many children it is impossible to do all the laundry that accumulates only when the moon is on the wane. Trusting in your powers of invention, you should at least try the experiment of putting off the bulk of the work until the waning moon. The results of this rearrangement will speak for themselves and awaken the inspiration to undertake further alterations in your working routine.

☾

Laundry will be cleaner if it is carried out when the moon is waning, especially on water days (preferably Pisces, but also Scorpio and Cancer).

The waxing moon leads to a heavy build-up of lather, and obstinate stains will stay behind in the item being washed.

☾

This rhythm—doing most of the laundry when the moon is waning—saves a lot of detergent; the fabric is preserved and lasts longer; obstinate stains are easier to remove.

Here is a tip for grease (especially car grease and bicycle oil stains): when the moon is waning, on a water day, rub in a little lard. Then wash normally.

Environmentally conscious people often find that some stains cannot be dealt with by means of natural methods. Such "gallant fighters" for a better environment will be especially glad to discover that paying attention to the phases of the moon can produce good results.

DRY CLEANING

Clothes that are valuable or mark easily—lambskin, leather, eider-downs, silk—should only be taken to the dry cleaners when the moon is *waning*. The fabric will come to no harm at that time, the garment will last longer, and the colors will not fade. If possible the sign of *Capricorn* should generally be avoided for dry cleaning—it causes the dreaded "sheen" to appear on garments.

Seasonal clothing in particular should only be washed or cleaned when the moon is on the wane, before it disappears into the wardrobe for six months or more.

WOODEN AND PARQUET FLOORS

Wooden floors should only be thoroughly scrubbed when the moon is *waning*. When the moon is waxing you should simply sweep the floor, or else mop it during a light sign. If you mop the floor during a water sign (Cancer, Scorpio, Pisces) while the moon is waxing, moisture can get in the cracks and eventually the wood may warp or even rot.

CLEANING WINDOWS AND GLASS

Often streaks and smears are left behind after windows have been cleaned, even when ethyl alcohol is used. However if you watch out for a light or warm day when the moon is waning, water with a dash of ethyl alcohol and some newspaper will be enough to give a clear view. Strong or concentrated substances are unnecessary.

Anyone who has ever tried to clean a smoke-stained computer or TV screen will know just how valuable this advice is. Incidentally, when cleaning extremely dirty window frames you achieve even better results on a watery day. It is well worth the wait.

Porcelain

The Chinese have always taken it for granted that one should not remove the dark coating that forms in their teapots (in any case they mostly use teapots made of black iron). They even say that the "soul" of the tea resides in this coating and every new cup adds a certain something, and this is what makes the brew "a real pot of tea."

Be that as it may, in many places it is considered unrefined to put a delicate porcelain teapot with such a layer in it on the tea table. This obstinate coating, and of course also lipstick and coffee stains and the like, can often be annoying, especially when attempts at cleaning leave behind fine scratches on the precious material, or the colors get "cleaned off." Those tormented with such things will take the following advice gratefully to heart:

℄

When the moon is waning take a wet cloth, put a little salt on it and polish the stained surface of the porcelain.

℄

When the moon is on the wane almost any gentle household remedy is helpful, whereas when the moon is waxing even aggressive scouring agents fail to produce the desired results and merely scratch the surface. The proof of the pudding is in the eating.

METALS

In many respects the situation is the same with metals as it is with porcelain: on some days the polishing agent scratches patterns into the gleaming surface; on other days it is enough to breathe on it and give it a wipe, and it's clean again.

Simply look out for the *waning* moon and use small quantities of mild household agents.

> *Brass*: when the moon is waning, stir equal parts of flour and salt with a little vinegar into a cream and apply thoroughly. Leave it for a short time to take effect, then wash it off and rub dry.
>
> *Silver*: when the moon is waning, on an air day, clean with diluted ammonia water and polish afterwards with a little French chalk.
>
> *Copper*: when the moon is waning, stir a little salt into some hot vinegar and clean with that. Rub it dry thoroughly afterwards.

SHOES

All sorts of footwear stay clean longer if they are polished when the moon is on the wane; the leather wears out less and lasts longer. Of course it's not possible only to clean shoes when the moon is waning; but obstinate dirt is easier to remove at that time. Particularly when winter boots are packed away in the cupboard, they should be cleaned and polished during the waning moon.

A first impregnation of waterproof coating on brand new shoes when the moon is waning will last practically the whole life of the shoes.

Mold

Modern, tightly shutting windows together with badly insulated walls have a serious disadvantage: the surfaces of the walls, especially in corners that let in the cold, can be a breeding ground for mold if the humidity is high. When the moon is *waning* it is much easier to combat this than when it is waxing; the effects last longer. Mild remedies, for instance vinegar and water, applied with a scrubbing brush, would be sufficient.

Spring Cleaning

Spring is the best breeding ground for a certain variety of bacillus: a strange restlessness seizes hold of the whole family and the lengthening days bring it to light. It's time for spring-cleaning! Attic and dining room, basement, and garage are all waiting to be thoroughly ransacked, aired, and cleaned.

Nature has arranged things that the best days for such work do in fact occur in spring (although there are alternatives almost as good throughout the whole year).

☽

For clearing out, airing, and cleaning, look for an air day when the moon is waning. Since air days are always followed by water days, you should not tackle the removal of stubborn dirt and thorough cleaning until after the "airier" tasks; i.e. wait until the water days.

☽

Early in the year the air sign *Aquarius* always comes when the moon is on the wane. These days would be ideal, because immediately afterwards the water sign Pisces supports all kinds of thorough cleaning.

EVERYTHING FROM AIRING
TO FAMILY OUTINGS

VENTILATION—BUT GET IT RIGHT!

Rooms: In this age of tightly shutting windows, rooms are not ventilated enough, especially in winter. This is perhaps understandable, since one might well get the idea that the air outside gives more cause for concern than the air indoors. And yet often precisely the reverse is the case: nowadays people even talk of "house sickness syndrome," a complex of illnesses caused by the poisonous vapors emanating from modern building materials, wood preservatives, and poorly functioning air-conditioning units. Regular ventilation is necessary and is always better than no ventilation at all.

☾

Ventilate generously on air and warmth days, briefly and rapidly on earth and water days.

☾

Beds: Airing beds seems to have gone out of fashion, at least in the town, where these days one can only rarely see colorful duvets and feather beds billowing out from windows and balconies. There will be various reasons for this: perhaps one does not want dust to blow into a neighbor's apartment on the floor below, or one doesn't like bringing feather beds back into the house damper than they were when they were hung out. For those inclined to rheumatism nothing could be worse.

And yet airing the bedding at the correct time is a good thing: the beds become fresh and fragrant and let the body breathe. Airing is also a good remedy against the dust mite, an allergenic microscopic animal that feeds on flakes of dead skin.

☾

Beds should be generously aired when the moon is on the wane in an air or fire sign. Only air briefly when the moon is waxing, otherwise too much moisture remains in the feathers. Avoid strong sunlight as this can damage the feathers. When there is no "r" in the month the bedding can be aired for a longer time.

☾

It should be noted that by "airing the beds" we do not mean the daily airing before the beds are made, but instead hanging the bedding from a window or balcony.

Mattresses: on average mattresses are kept in use for much too long (ten years or more). Well, if that's the situation, then at least they should be regularly cleaned and above all aired. Airing them drives away the dust mites, which can only thrive in a moist, warm climate.

☾

Mattresses should be cleaned and aired when the moon is waning, preferably on an air day or a warmth day. This protects against vermin and draws out moisture (important for people with rheumatism or allergies). Under no circumstances should they be aired on a water day when the moon is waxing. This attracts damp and would be extremely bad for rheumatic people. Earth days are not especially suitable, either.

☾

Storing Away Summer and Winter Clothes

Mothballs have had their day, it has to be said; but for anyone who is mistrustful about odorless anti-moth paper steeped in poisons and similar things, here is a well-tried remedy:

☾

Hang your summer or winter clothing away in the closet in autumn or spring on an air day when the moon is waning. Anti-moth preparations will then be superfluous.

☾

As an alternative the ascending moon is also a possibility. Clothing stored away on earth days can take on a strong smell and even go moldy; if it is stored away on a water day it will become damp.

Preserving, Bottling, and Storing

Nowadays homemade jam and home-preserved vegetables and fruit are all the rage. The most important rules for successful harvesting, storing, and preserving have already been presented in Chapter 3.

A favorable time for making jam and juices is the *ascending moon*. The fruit is much juicier and the aroma is much better, too. It will keep much longer and you will often be able to dispense with artificial setting agents (this also applies to the preserving and bottling of other foods). Just try it out: one time using your usual method and then on another occasion with less preserving sugar—say half the amount (or you can use apples)—but at the right time.

THE MOON AS A "HELPER" IN THE HOME AND EVERYDAY LIFE

☾

The most favorable time for making preserves is the period of the ascending moon (Sagittarius to Gemini). Preserving, bottling, and storing is thus less dependent on the phases of the moon than on the star sign through which the moon is currently passing.

The best time for gathering and preserving fruit is Aries (a fruit day). For root vegetables it is Capricorn and Taurus (root days).

Fruit and vegetables keep better if they are frozen on a fruit day rather than on water days. They taste better when defrosted, do not become so watery, and do not disintegrate. The cellar shelves for storing fruit should only be cleaned when the moon is on the wane (in an air or fire sign). This keeps them dry and prevents the musty smell that can often occur.

☾

BAKING BREAD

Baking bread is most successful when the moon is waning on a flower day (Gemini, Libra, Aquarius). It will keep much better at this time, too.

Here are a few more tips for baking bread with leaven that you can try out:

- ∿ When the moon is waning the dough generally rises more heavily. On the other hand when the moon is waxing it rises better; additional yeast is not needed at that time.

🐦 Baking during Aries, Leo, and Sagittarius produces better results; during Cancer, Scorpio, and Pisces the results are somewhat worse.

🐦 What is important when baking is that the oven should be preheated to a high temperature, after which the heat is slowly allowed to decrease.

Make an experiment: do one batch of baking when the moon is on the wane in Pisces, and another with the moon waxing in Leo. Then look at the difference.

Painting and Varnishing

Many highly poisonous and costly paints, emulsions, and varnishes were only able to gain acceptance at the expense of gentler lime wash paints and naturally produced varnishes because they literally overran the subtle influences of the natural rhythms.

The return to nature would certainly be easier in this area if nontoxic paints were always used at the correct moment. In terms of effectiveness and durability they are scarcely inferior to or just as good as today's fast-working poison brews. This is particularly true of interior wall paint.

☾

For all painting and varnishing tasks the period of the waning moon is most suitable. Paint and undercoat dry well and form beautiful surfaces. The paints combine well with the undercoat: the brush glides along almost by itself. Lime wash paint allows the undercoat to breathe.

Water days are unsuitable because the paint does not dry well. Leo days are also unsuitable because the drying effect is too strong and sometimes causes the paint to crack.

☾

Heating the House in Autumn

Every autumn the day finally comes when your own four walls need warming up, because the power of the sun is no longer sufficient to do this. In order to achieve a thorough and rapid warming of the whole house, the following rule should be observed:

☾

The first heating in autumn should take place on a warmth day (Aries, Leo, or Sagittarius) when the moon is waning.

☾

This advice is particularly important for a *new building*, which should without fail be heated for the first time at the times specified above. This will drive the last dampness from the walls.

Winter Windows

In modern mobile homes, and also in many old buildings and frequently in the country, removable double windows are found, which are stored away during summer in the cellar or the attic and are only brought out again in autumn to fulfill their heat-insulating function.

The time you select to replace them has a bearing on whether they continually steam or mist up throughout the winter. Anyone who prefers a clear view to a film of mist should pay attention to the following:

❦

Winter or inner windows should be fitted during the air signs (Aquarius or Gemini).

❦

In this way one can steer clear of undesirable side effects. This rule is also of interest to those building "ecologically sound" houses, for these times would produce equally beneficial effects when fitting windows in a new building.

THE CARE OF HOUSEPLANTS

Detailed instructions are already contained in Chapter 3 concerning the care of our green and colorful fellow lodgers. The more important ones are highlighted here once more:

❦

Re-potting and new planting of houseplants and balcony plants is best done during Virgo days. The plants will rapidly put down roots.

Watering should take place whenever possible only on leaf days (Cancer, Scorpio, Pisces), and definitely with rainwater or water that has stood for a long time. Taking houseplants out of doors in order to expose them to rain is sometimes harmful, because the leaves are not used to direct wetting.

Fertilizer should only be put down when the moon is on the wane, preferably on leaf days. Now and then on root days, too, if the root formation is weak, or on flower days if the plants in question are blooms that are unexpectedly sparing with their color.

❦

All the rules for combating pests (see Chapter 3) also apply here. Remember not to water too often on flower days, so as not to attract pests. Only pour organic pesticides over the root area, not on the stem, leaves, and flowers.

DAY QUALITY AND EXCURSIONS

Who does not enjoy an outing into the countryside now and then, whether alone, with a companion, or with family and friends?

Have you ever noticed that even with the *same* outdoor temperatures excursion days "feel" different—that we sometimes reach without thinking for our sunglasses even though the sky is cloudy, or that on one occasion we like to sit in the grass while on another we don't even bother to get out of our picnic chair because the ground feels unpleasantly damp or cold?

In this connection an example occurs to me: something that often happened to me as a boy years ago, when for many summer days in a row I used to go for rides on my first bicycle. With my pocket money I bought myself a drinking bottle—one of those plastic things that you fix to the frame and can then drink from during the journey. I would be on the road with my friends for hours, and was always surprised to find that—with the same temperature conditions—the contents of the bottle sometimes would be all gone after an hour, while on other occasions I would bring the bottle home in the evening still half-full.

This puzzle is solved if one briefly examines the four "day qualities"—particular characteristics of a day linked with the sign of the zodiac that is currently in force.

Warmth days prevail when the moon is in the signs Aries, Leo, and Sagittarius. These are generally good days for an outing, and they feel warm even if the sky is cloudy. They have a drying effect, particularly in Leo, and on these days you will perhaps feel thirstier than usual. In Leo days there often lurks the danger of strong storms suddenly brewing up, with harmful consequences especially after long heat waves—accompanied by hailstorms and floods (because the earth is unable to absorb enough moisture).

Light days or air days prevail when the moon is in Gemini, Libra, or Aquarius. At this time the earth and the plants collect more light than usual, and the effect on human beings is generally very pleasant. Car drivers occasionally find these days uncomfortable: even when the sky is cloudy people sometimes feel the need to wear sunglasses, as the light is felt to be piercing. Sportsmen, too, such as tennis players, sometimes find such light days unpleasant, if they have to serve into the sun—even if it is not shining directly into their eyes.

Cold days or earth days are Taurus, Virgo, and Capricorn. Even if the thermometer is registering very high temperatures, one should always take slightly warmer clothes and blankets, in case the sun disappears behind the clouds. The earth feels cold to the touch, and sometimes one will get goose bumps even if the tiniest fleecy cloud passes in front of the sun. On these days you will probably come home with your drinks basket half-full.

Wetness days (or water days)—Cancer, Scorpio, and Pisces—never allow the ground to dry out completely. The tendency to precipitation is greater, too. If possible don't leave home without waterproof clothing or an umbrella, and maybe even a blanket, if you are planning to go somewhere on a picnic or to lie down on the ground after bathing. Here's a tip: if you want to be better prepared for sudden changes in the weather or changes in climate, then watch out for new moon and full moon, and Gemini and Sagittarius days.

CARE OF THE BODY

THE KNOWLEDGE OF the lunar cycles can also be usefully applied to care of the body. However, one should bear in mind that the condition of skin, hair, and nails is almost always an indicator and symptom of a person's general state of health. Without "beauty from within," above all without a healthy diet, measures to take care of the body are frequently just cosmetic: they cover up the true causes of pale, fatty, or blemished skin, or of brittle nails.

The numerous tips and suggestions for a healthy way of life in Chapter 2 are at the same time a great help in working from within to produce healthy skin and strong hair—especially because you will then be able to save a lot of money on what are often extremely expensive cosmetic procedures.

SKIN CARE

By skin care we do not mean daily washing or the application of skin cream, but instead dealing with problematic skin conditions, for instance by means of special face packs or masks. This is best carried out when the moon is *waning*—particularly when minor "operations" to deal with bumps, pimples, and so on are necessary: scars almost never form when the moon is on the wane. Skin specialists could avoid many problems if they would set flexible appointments in this period.

On the other hand, if substances are being supplied to the skin, for instance by means of firming or moisturizing creams, then the phases of the *waxing* moon is more suitable.

Anyone who wishes in addition to take the sign of zodiac into account shouldn't miss the *Capricorn* days. They are appropriate for every kind of skin care.

HAIR CARE

Many preparations for hair and dandruff would be superfluous if you were to observe the correct times for hair treatment. Formerly no one was surprised if a barber closed his shop on certain days, because people knew that no one would be availing themselves of his services anyway. On the other hand if Leo fell on a Sunday many people would seek him out after church and entrust their hair to him.

In my home in Tyrol there used to be very few men with bald heads. Perhaps the reason for that was from a baby's very first haircut people always looked out for a Leo day.

☾

Leo days and Virgo days are haircut days—regardless of whether the moon is waning or waxing.

On Pisces and Cancer days one should try not to get a haircut.

☾

For anyone who is unhappy about his or her hair, because for instance it is falling out, too thin, or too greasy, we recommend this "cure," which will not fail to be effective:

🐦 Have your hair cut or trimmed every month *from February to August on Leo days*. During that period Leo always occurs in the waxing moon, which further reinforces the good effect. The Leo quality has a special effect on male hormones; perhaps that is an explanation for the "hairy" effect of Leo days, i.e., for the fact that hair becomes stronger.

❧ Once or twice a week during this time whisk one or two eggs (yolk *and* white) and massage it into the hair after washing. Leave it for a short while to take effect, then rinse it out with warm water.

❧ It is important that the final rinse is carried out with cold water. The temperature is right when the water feels cold on the head. Actually this rule should always be followed, even if one has strong, healthy hair.

❧ Do not use a hair drier during this time. However, if this is absolutely necessary, wait for a quarter of an hour. Never blow-dry in the "wrong" direction, or at too high a temperature: in the long run that will destroy all the hair.

However cutting hair exclusively on Leo days is not a certain remedy for falling hair, because we often lose hair as a result of the effects of medicines, hormonal changes, and the concomitant emotional upheaval. Especially after pregnancy or during the change of life, there is an increased occurrence of hair loss, but later this subsides again.

Hair that is cut during *Virgo* retains its form and beauty longer. Virgo is especially suitable for permanent waves; during Leo days these become too frizzy.

A haircut on *Pisces* days frequently leads to dandruff. If the hair is cut during *Cancer* it becomes shaggy and unmanageable.

If possible you should therefore also avoid washing your hair on *Pisces* and *Cancer* days. Many people, particularly young people, wash their hair practically every day; but in youth the body can put up with more. Later you may well wish to start taking this advice to heart.

If for any reason you should wish to say goodbye to bodily hair, then choose the time of the waning moon to remove it. For this purpose one should not miss *Capricorn when the moon is on the wane* (only during the first six months of the year). Just at that time the hair will not grow back so rapidly. However, you should not go too far with eyebrow-plucking.

NAIL CARE

If they are cut at the correct time, fingernails and toenails become hard, robust, and do not break so easily. Special preparations for the nails are superfluous, since in any case they combat the symptom and not the cause. The rule runs as follows:

☽

For the care of toenails and fingernails, for cutting and filing the most suitable times are Capricorn and any Friday after sunset.

☽

The tip that you should care for your nails on Friday evenings will perhaps raise a smile at first; but my grandfather, from whom I received this knowledge, used to swear by this rule and also said this was why he never had toothache. At any rate he lived to be 89 and in his whole life never had problems with his teeth. I also followed this rule, together with my family, and can only confirm the connection. If you try it out, the good results will speak for themselves.

Guitarists are among the few people who have to attend to their nails very frequently. At the very least they should steer clear of unfavorable influences and dispense with nail-care on the first day of *Pisces* (directly after Aquarius) and on one of the two or three *Gemini* days.

Ingrown nails should never be corrected or cut when the moon is *waning*, otherwise they always grow back wrong. The exception to this is correction of the nail-bed: this minor operation is more successful when carried out during the waning moon (avoiding Pisces if possible). Incidentally the treatment of obstinate athlete's foot and nail fungus is likewise effective when the moon is on the wane. The same applies to warts as well.

The feet are a very important and sensitive part of the body; they regrettably receive much too shabby treatment from many people. If the foot is ill, the human being is ill. Every area of the body is reflected in the reflex zones of the feet and can be influenced by *reflex zone massage*. If these regions are to be stimulated to break something down, e.g., to remove tension or poison from the body, then the period of the waning moon is more favorable. However, if the effect is intended to be restorative, e.g., regeneration and strengthening of bodily functions, then the period of the waxing moon is more favorable.

MASSAGES

A skilled massage is not only soothing but also a very good preventive measure against illnesses of all kinds. It has a relaxing and stabilizing effect on the heart and circulation, stimulates the activity of the organs, and in particular can be very helpful for people with blood pressure problems.

When illnesses are actually present then special massages such as lymph drainage can be particularly conducive to healing and decongesting. However, they should only be carried out by experienced physiotherapists.

❦

For massages that serve to relax, ease tension, and detox-
ify, the most suitable time is when the moon is waning.
If a massage is intended to have a mainly regenerating
and strengthening effect, perhaps with the aid of appropriate
oils, it will achieve better results when the moon is waxing.

❦

Of course massages subsequent to inflammations and injuries, lymph drainage and the like cannot and should not wait for the "correct" moment—on the contrary. Waiting can cause great damage that outweighs the good effect of the massage given in keeping with the lunar cycle. The above directions thus apply principally to people who are in good health.

In the course of conversations with my brother, Georg Koller, who has a physiotherapy practice in Osnabrück, Germany, and who is also familiar with the lunar rhythms, I have learned about the great success of special massages and how they are applied. As a physio-therapist and chiropractor he tries to carry out difficult treatments at the correct moment.

THE FEET

The feet are a very important and sensitive part of the body and are regrettably often neglected by many people. If our feet are not healthy, this manifests itself in our general well-being. Every area of the body is reflected in the reflex zones of the feet and can be influenced by reflexology massage. In a similar manner to acupres-sure (pressure on particular points throughout the whole of the body) it is possible through well-directed pressure and friction to arouse these zones and thereby to flood the relevant organs and regions of the body with energy and stimulate them to function normally. Reflex zone massage is even suitable as a diagnostic instrument. Generally those points on the foot whose corresponding organs are debilitated are more painful or even identifiable by a thick callus. Thus with poor footwear we harm not only our feet but also our whole body.

The rules for the ideal time to carry out this type of massage are the same as those for massage in general. The force of Pisces days greatly assists the effect of this form of massage. On these days one should carry out massage with special care, because people are more sensitive then. Anyone going to a medical practitioner or masseur for a reflex zone massage for the first time is probably well advised to steer clear of Pisces days. Reflex zone massages intended to stimulate organs of detoxification are generally more effective during the waning than during the waxing moon.

For the Future

☾

ALL THE RULES in this book derive their validity from intuition and perception—not arbitrary whim, supposition, theory, or faith. Sharpened senses, alertness, and precise observation of nature and of oneself made our ancestors masters of the art of lunar timing.

Consider this: It would never have been possible to receive this knowledge and successfully pass it on again and again, if each succeeding generation had just followed the rules without grasping their meaning, without at the same time possessing itself of the awareness which confirms the validity of these rules and allows them to become flesh and blood—*without* always having to refer to a handbook or call on the services of experts. There is no law in the world that can continue to exist more than a couple of decades if it is not rooted in the reality of nature and mankind.

The position of the moon is merely the hand of a clock. The feeling for what it indicates is something that we bear within us. This book is ultimately only an aid to reawakening this awareness and regaining confidence in it—to having the courage to hearken to it. This knowledge is valid and relevant everywhere on earth, but one has to grow with it organically. Our fields, like our bodies, have had to get used to so much negativity: the return to the natural, to harmony with the rhythms of nature, demands time.

The lunar cycles can be of service to you at any time if you familiarize yourself with a characteristic of nature: She works slowly, at her own tempo, and she will not let herself be hurried. If you keep this aspect in view, the knowledge of the lunar rhythms will make itself accessible to you of its own accord.

This book is merely a tool, not a patent remedy. How you wield this tool is left entirely to you.

Appendix A

℃

HERBS, PLANTS, AND TREES MENTIONED IN THE TEXT

★ An asterisk indicates that the name refers to a number of related species.

English	Latin
Alder	*Rhamnus frangula*
Balm	*Melissa officinalis*
Basil	*Ocimum basilicum*
Birch	*Betula*★
Bramble	*Rubus fruticosus*
Chamomile	*Matricaria recutita*
Charlock	*Sinapis arvensis*
Chive	*Allium schoenoprasum*
Coltsfoot	*Tussilago farfara*
Comfrey	*Symphytum officinale*
Common buckthorn	*Rhamnus catharticus*
Common clubmoss	*Lycopodium clavatum*
Cornflower	*Centaurea cyanus*
Cowslip	*Primula veris*

Daisy	*Bellis perennis*
Dandelion	*Taraxacum officinale*
Dead-nettle	*Lamium* ★
Elder	*Sambucus nigra*
Eyebright	*Euphrasia officinalis*
Fennel	*Foeniculum vulgare*
Fumitory	*Fumaria officinalis*
Garlic	*Allium sativum*
Greater celandine	*Chelidonium majus*
Heartsease	*Viola tricolor*
Heather	*Caluna vulgaris*
Horsetail	*Equisetum arvense*
Lady's mantle	*Alchemilla* ★
Laurel	*Laurus nobilis*
Liverwort	*Hepaticae* ★
Lovage	*Levisticum officinale*
Marigold	*Calendula officinalis*
Marjoram	*Origanum vulgare*
Mistletoe	*Viscum album*
Mugwort	*Artemisia vulgaris*
Mullein	*Verbascum thapsus*
Nasturtium	*Tropaeolum majus*
Parsley	*Petroselinum crispum*
Ribbed melilot	*Melilotus officinalis*
Rosemary	*Rosmarinus officinalis*
Sage	*Salvia officinalis*

Senna	*Cassia*★
Shepherd's purse	*Capsella bursa-pastoris*
Speedwell	*Veronica officinalis*
St. John's wort	*Hypericum perforatum*
Stinging nettle	*Urtica dioica*
Sweet chestnut	*Castanea sativa*
Sweet woodruff	*Asperula odorata*
Tansy	*Chrysanthemum vulgare*
Thyme	*Thymus vulgaris*
Violet	*Viola*★
Watercress	*Nasturtium officinale*
Wild radish	*Raphanus raphanistrum*
Willow	*Salix*★
Wood garlic, ramson	*Allium ursinum*
Wormwood	*Artemisia absinthium*
Yarrow	*Achillea millefolium*
Yellow gentian	*Gentiana lutea*

Afterword

CORRESPONDENCE WITH THE authors, inquiries for lectures and discussions should be addressed to:

Johanna Paungger / Thomas Poppe
Post Box 107
A—3400 Klosterneuburg
Austria

We shall endeavor to answer all inquiries, but ask for your understanding if because of the avalanche of letters from many countries we are unable to give any guarantee of this. We are sincerely grateful for the confidence in our work that is expressed in such letters and would like to say a few words here in reply that may be of some use to you.

There are many inquiries to which we are unable to reply, for the simple reason that we do not know the answer. We are only writing from personal experience, and there are limits to that. This is especially true of physical and mental disorders: we are not doctors and we have no right—nor any wish—to presume to make judgments from a distance as to what is beneficial or harmful in a particular case.

We have received numerous requests for the addresses of good dowsers or healers who work according to lunar and natural cycles. There are admittedly more of these every day, but all the ones that we know have now become hopelessly overstretched because their work is so successful. It is very simple: if the doctor of your choice is unwilling to go along with your wishes, then find another one. A really good doctor will always do everything to ensure that you get well and stay well. On the other hand, anyone who works exclusively according to book-learning and fixed patterns is either only interested in earning money, or else he is ignoring his own experience: namely, that statistics and patterns learned by rote never cover the individual case.

A large proportion of the letters contained inquiries about sources for particular services or products in fields related to our work, such as wood cut at the right time or natural teas and cosmetics produced in harmony with lunar rhythms. With the aim of coping with at least some of these requests, we looked for possible partners and companies in order to help interested readers. Our success can be studied in a little German "moonshop" catalogue we're willing to send you upon request. Experience nevertheless showed us that our aim could only be realized with the greatest difficulty: first, many companies have become overextended and are fully booked up. Second, in the course of time the orientation of many of them has shifted away from service to the customer and toward the greatest possible economic success. However, this rules out any close collaboration with us. There is nothing basically wrong with money and economic success: what really matters is the way people handle these things. We take pleasure in economic success but never make it the goal of our work.

Many readers ask questions that have already been answered in the books, or which, with careful reading and patience, could be derived from the numerous basic rules. Our answer would only obstruct the pleasure and long-term profit to be gained from personal experience. The entire thrust of our second book is that our readers have to take the initiative and assume responsibility for their own health.

Most of the letters are ultimately about problems that the readers are asking us for our personal help in solving. And yet almost always the solution to the problem is already waiting just outside the door. Often the only reason why it is not allowed in is because in the search for it one has become obsessed by a certain direction and is then too proud, anxious, or lazy to take a different tack.

Our entire work, both now and in the future, is directed toward awakening in people the courage to make their own decisions and take responsibility for themselves—the courage to get right to the bottom of a problem, look at it from every side and think things through to the end. There is no other person, no "expert" who can take on this task for you—and that goes for us, too. If our work has been able to awaken in you the courage to do this, then we rejoice with you from the bottom of our hearts.

Index

varnishing, 204-5
vegetables, 46, 122-23, 141, 145,
        148-50
    see also plants
ventilation, 200-1
vermin. *see* pests
vernal equinox, 21
Virgo, 25, 90, 98, 139-42, 153-54

W

waning moon, 10-11, 38, 76, 117
warmth days, **40**, 42, 208
warts, 74-75
water days, **40**, 42, 208
watercourse management, 166-67
waxing moon, 9-10, 38, 76, 117
weaning, 75, 171
weather conditions, 95
weeds, 60, 125-35, 164
weight, 38-39
windows and glass, 196-97, 205-6
Winterswyl, Ricarda: *Sddeutsche
        Zeitung*, 6, 125
wood, 172-88
    for bridges and boats, 185-86
    for building and floors, 185-86

cutting, xii
felling and cutting, 172-80
for fires, 184
for furniture, 181
grubbing and clearing, 180-81
non-inflammable, 182-83
non-rotting, 182
non-shrinking, 184
non-splitting, 186-87
for planks and sawing, 185
for tools, 181

Z

zodiac
    and agriculture, 127-42, 149-
        57
    constellations of, 4
    and gardening, 115-20
    and health, 89-103, **90**
    impulse characteristics of, **115**
    and medicinal herbs, 63-65, **64**
    moon in the, 11-15, **16**
    and parts of the body, 15-18
    position of moon and, 8-9
zodiacal table, **25**

Moon Calendar
2003-2010

☾

♈ = Aries		♎ = Libra
♉ = Taurus		♏ = Scorpio
♊ = Gemini		♐ = Sagittarius
♋ = Cancer		♑ = Capricorn
♌ = Leo		♒ = Aquarius
♍ = Virgo		♓ = Pisces

☺ = Full Moon
☾ = Waning Moon
● = New Moon
☽ = Waxing Moon

M = Monday
T = Tuesday.
W = Wednesday
T = Thursday
F = Friday
S = Saturday
S = Sunday

2003

January
W	1	
T	2	●
F	3	
S	4	
S	5	
M	6	
T	7	
W	8	
T	9	
F	10	)
S	11	
S	12	
M	13	
T	14	
W	15	
T	16	
F	17	
S	18	☺
S	19	
M	20	
T	21	
W	22	
T	23	
F	24	
S	25	C
S	26	
M	27	
T	28	
W	29	
T	30	
F	31	

February
S	1	●
S	2	
M	3	
T	4	
W	5	
T	6	
F	7	
S	8	
S	9	)
M	10	
T	11	
W	12	
T	13	
F	14	
S	15	
S	16	
M	17	☺
T	18	
W	19	
T	20	
F	21	
S	22	
S	23	C
M	24	
T	25	
W	26	
T	27	
F	28	

March
S	1	
S	2	
M	3	●
T	4	
W	5	
T	6	
F	7	
S	8	
S	9	
M	10	
T	11	)
W	12	
T	13	
F	14	
S	15	
S	16	
M	17	
T	18	☺
W	19	
T	20	
F	21	
S	22	
S	23	
M	24	
T	25	C
W	26	
T	27	
F	28	
S	29	
S	30	
M	31	

April
T	1	●
W	2	
T	3	
F	4	
S	5	
S	6	
M	7	
T	8	
W	9	
T	10	)
F	11	
S	12	
S	13	
M	14	
T	15	
W	16	☺
T	17	
F	18	
S	19	
S	20	
M	21	
T	22	
W	23	C
T	24	
F	25	
S	26	
S	27	
M	28	
T	29	
W	30	

May
T	1	●
F	2	
S	3	
S	4	
M	5	
T	6	
W	7	
T	8	
F	9	)
S	10	
S	11	
M	12	
T	13	
W	14	
T	15	
F	16	☺
S	17	
S	18	
M	19	
T	20	
W	21	
T	22	
F	23	C
S	24	
S	25	
M	26	
T	27	
W	28	
T	29	
F	30	
S	31	●

June
S	1	
M	2	
T	3	
W	4	
T	5	
F	6	
S	7	)
S	8	
M	9	
T	10	
W	11	
T	12	
F	13	
S	14	☺
S	15	
M	16	
T	17	
W	18	
T	19	
F	20	
S	21	C
S	22	
M	23	
T	24	
W	25	
T	26	
F	27	
S	28	
S	29	●
M	30	

2003

July

T	1
W	2
T	3
F	4
S	5
S	6
M	7 ☽
T	8
W	9
T	10
F	11
S	12
S	13 ☺
M	14
T	15
W	16
T	17
F	18
S	19
S	20
M	21 ☾
T	22
W	23
T	24
F	25
S	26
S	27
M	28
T	29 ●
W	30
T	31

August

F	1
S	2
S	3
M	4
T	5 ☽
W	6
T	7
F	8
S	9
S	10
M	11
T	12 ☺
W	13
T	14
F	15
S	16
S	17
M	18
T	19
W	20 ☾
T	21
F	22
S	23
S	24
M	25
T	26
W	27 ●
T	28
F	29 ●
S	30
S	31

September

M	1
T	2
W	3 ☽
T	4
F	5
S	6
S	7
M	8
T	9
W	10 ☺
T	11
F	12
S	13
S	14
M	15
T	16
W	17
T	18 ☾
F	19
S	20
S	21
M	22
T	23
W	24
T	25
F	26 ●
S	27
S	28
M	29
T	30

October

W	1
T	2 ☽
F	3
S	4
S	5
M	6
T	7
W	8
T	9 ☺
F	10 ☺
S	11
S	12
M	13
T	14
W	15
T	16
F	17
S	18 ☾
S	19
M	20
T	21
W	22
T	23
F	24
S	25 ●
S	26
M	27
T	28
W	29
T	30
F	31

November

S	1 ☽
S	2
M	3
T	4
W	5
T	6
F	7
S	8
S	9 ☺
M	10
T	11
W	12
T	13
F	14
S	15
S	16
M	17 ☾
T	18
W	19
T	20
F	21
S	22
S	23
M	24 ●
T	25
W	26
T	27
F	28
S	29
S	30 ☽

December

M	1
T	2
W	3
T	4
F	5
S	6
S	7
M	8 ☺
T	9
W	10
T	11
F	12
S	13
S	14
M	15
T	16 ☾
W	17
T	18
F	19
S	20
S	21
M	22
T	23 ●
W	24
T	25
F	26
S	27
S	28
M	29
T	30 ☽
W	31

2004

January	February	March	April	May	June
T 1	S 1	M 1	T 1	S 1	T 1
F 2		T 2	F 2	S 2	W 2
S 3	M 2	W 3	S 3		T 3 ☺
S 4	T 3	T 4	S 4	M 3	F 4
	W 4	F 5		T 4 ☺	S 5
M 5	T 5	S 6	M 5 ☺	W 5	S 6
T 6	F 6 ☺	S 7 ☺	T 6	T 6	
W 7 ☺	S 7		W 7	F 7	M 7
T 8	S 8	M 8	T 8	S 8	T 8
F 9		T 9	F 9	S 9	W 9 (
S 10	M 9	W 10	S 10		T 10
S 11	T 10	T 11	S 11	M 10	F 11
	W 11	F 12		T 11 (	S 12
M 12	T 12	S 13 (	M 12 (	W 12	S 13
T 13	F 13 (	S 14	T 13	T 13	
W 14	S 14		W 14	F 14	M 14
T 15 (	S 15	M 15	T 15	S 15	T 15
F 16		T 16	F 16	S 16	W 16
S 17	M 16	W 17	S 17		T 17 ●
S 18	T 17	T 18	S 18	M 17	F 18
	W 18	F 19		T 18	S 19
M 19	T 19	S 20 ●	M 19 ●	W 19 ●	S 20
T 20	F 20 ●	S 21	T 20	T 20	
W 21 ●	S 21		W 21	F 21	M 21
T 22	S 22	M 22	T 22	S 22	T 22
F 23		T 23	F 23	S 23	W 23
S 24	M 23	W 24	S 24		T 24
S 25	T 24	T 25	S 25	M 24	F 25)
	W 25	F 26		T 25)	S 26
M 26	T 26	S 27	M 26	W 26	S 27
T 27	F 27	S 28	T 27)	T 27	
W 28	S 28)		W 28	F 28	M 28
T 29)	S 29	M 29)	T 29	S 29	T 29
F 30		T 30	F 30	S 30	W 30
S 31		W 31		M 31	

2004

July			August			September			October			November			December		
T	1		S	1		W	1		F	1		M	1		W	1	
F	2	☺				T	2		S	2		T	2		T	2	
S	3		M	2		F	3		S	3		W	3		F	3	
S	4		T	3		S	4					T	4		S	4	
			W	4		S	5		M	4		F	5	☾	S	5	☾
M	5		T	5					T	5		S	6				
T	6		F	6		M	6	☾	W	6	☾	S	7		M	6	
W	7		S	7	☾	T	7		T	7					T	7	
T	8		S	8		W	8		F	8		M	8		W	8	
F	9	☾				T	9		S	9		T	9		T	9	
S	10		M	9		F	10		S	10		W	10		F	10	
S	11		T	10		S	11					T	11		S	11	
			W	11		S	12		M	11		F	12	●	S	12	●
M	12		T	12					T	12		S	13				
T	13		F	13		M	13		W	13		S	14		M	13	
W	14		S	14		T	14	●	T	14	●				T	14	
T	15		S	15		W	15		F	15		M	15		W	15	
F	16					T	16		S	16		T	16		T	16	
S	17	●	M	16	●	F	17		S	17		W	17		F	17	
S	18		T	17		S	18					T	18		S	18	☽
			W	18		S	19		M	18		F	19	☽	S	19	
M	19		T	19					T	19		S	20				
T	20		F	20		M	20		W	20	☽	S	21		M	20	
W	21		S	21		T	21	☽	T	21					T	21	
T	22		S	22		W	22		F	22		M	22		W	22	
F	23					T	23		S	23		T	23		T	23	
S	24		M	23	☽	F	24		S	24		W	24		F	24	
S	25	☽	T	24		S	25					T	25		S	25	
			W	25		S	26		M	25		F	26	☺	S	26	☺
M	26		T	26					T	26		S	27				
T	27		F	27		M	27		W	27		S	28		M	27	
W	28		S	28		T	28	☺	T	28	☺				T	28	
T	29		S	29		W	29		F	29		M	29		W	29	
F	30					T	30		S	30		T	30		T	30	
S	31	☺	M	30	☺				S	31					F	31	
			T	31													

2005

January	February	March	April	May	June
S 1	T 1	T 1	F 1 🌒	S 1 🌒	W 1
S 2	W 2 🌒	W 2	S 2 🌒	M 2	T 2
M 3 🌒	T 3	T 3 🌒	S 3	T 3	F 3
T 4	F 4	F 4		W 4	S 4
W 5	S 5	S 5	M 4	T 5	S 5
T 6	S 6	S 6	T 5	F 6	
F 7			W 6	S 7	M 6 ●
S 8	M 7	M 7	T 7	S 8 ●	T 7
S 9	T 8 ●	T 8	F 8 ●		W 8
	W 9	W 9	S 9	M 9	T 9
M 10 ●	T 10	T 10 ●	S 10	T 10	F 10
T 11	F 11	F 11		W 11	S 11
W 12	S 12	S 12	M 11	T 12	S 12
T 13	S 13	S 13	T 12	F 13	
F 14			W 13	S 14	M 13
S 15	M 14	M 14	T 14	S 15	T 14
S 16	T 15	T 15	F 15		W 15 🌓
	W 16 🌓	W 16	S 16 🌓	M 16 🌓	T 16
M 17 🌓	T 17	T 17 🌓	S 17	T 17	F 17
T 18	F 18	F 18		W 18	S 18
W 19	S 19	S 19	M 18	T 19	S 19
T 20	S 20	S 20	T 19	F 20	
F 21			W 20	S 21	M 20
S 22	M 21	M 21	T 21	S 22	T 21
S 23	T 22	T 22	F 22		W 22 ☺
	W 23	W 23	S 23	M 23 ☺	T 23
M 24	T 24 ☺	T 24	S 24 ☺	T 24	F 24
T 25 ☺	F 25	F 25 ☺		W 25	S 25
W 26	S 26	S 26	M 25	T 26	S 26
T 27	S 27	S 27	T 26	F 27	
F 28			W 27	S 28	M 27
S 29	M 28	M 28	T 28	S 29	T 28 🌒
S 30		T 29	F 29		W 29
		W 30	S 30	M 30 🌒	T 30
M 31		T 31		T 31	

2005

July	August	September	October	November	December
F 1	M 1	T 1	S 1	T 1	T 1 ●
S 2	T 2	F 2	S 2	W 2 ●	F 2
S 3	W 3	S 3 ●	—	T 3	S 3
—	T 4	S 4	M 3 ●	F 4	S 4
M 4	F 5 ●	—	T 4	S 5	—
T 5	S 6	M 5	W 5	S 6	M 5
W 6 ●	S 7	T 6	T 6	—	T 6
T 7	—	W 7	F 7	M 7	W 7
F 8	M 8	T 8	S 8	T 8	T 8 ☽
S 9	T 9	F 9	S 9	W 9 ☽	F 9
S 10	W 10	S 10	—	T 10	S 10
—	T 11	S 11 ☽	M 10 ☽	F 11	S 11
M 11	F 12	—	T 11	S 12	—
T 12	S 13 ☽	M 12	W 12	S 13	M 12
W 13	S 14	T 13	T 13	—	T 13
T 14 ☽	—	W 14	F 14	M 14	W 14
F 15	M 15	T 15	S 15	T 15	T 15 ☺
S 16	T 16	F 16	S 16	W 16 ☺	F 16
S 17	W 17	S 17	—	T 17	S 17
—	T 18	S 18 ☺	M 17 ☺	F 18	S 18
M 18	F 19 ☺	—	T 18	S 19	—
T 19	S 20	M 19	W 19	S 20	M 19
W 20	S 21	T 20	T 20	—	T 20
T 21 ☺	—	W 21	F 21	M 21	W 21
F 22	M 22	T 22	S 22	T 22	T 22
S 23	T 23	F 23	S 23	W 23 ☾	F 23 ☾
S 24	W 24	S 24	—	T 24	S 24
—	T 25	S 25 ☾	M 24	F 25	S 25
M 25	F 26 ☾	—	T 25 ☾	S 26	—
T 26	S 27	M 26	W 26	S 27	M 26
W 27	S 28	T 27	T 27	—	T 27
T 28 ☾	—	W 28	F 28	M 28	W 28
F 29	M 29	T 29	S 29	T 29	T 29
S 30	T 30	F 30	S 30	W 30	F 30
S 31	W 31	—	M 31	—	S 31 ●

2006

January
- S 1
- M 2
- T 3
- W 4
- T 5
- F 6 ☽
- S 7
- S 8
- M 9
- T 10
- W 11
- T 12
- F 13
- S 14 ☺
- S 15
- M 16
- T 17
- W 18
- T 19
- F 20
- S 21
- S 22 ☾
- M 23
- T 24
- W 25
- T 26
- F 27
- S 28
- S 29 ●
- M 30
- T 31

February
- W 1
- T 2
- F 3
- S 4
- S 5 ☽
- M 6
- T 7
- W 8
- T 9
- F 10
- S 11
- S 12
- M 13 ☺
- T 14
- W 15
- T 16
- F 17
- S 18
- S 19
- M 20
- T 21 ☾
- W 22
- T 23
- F 24
- S 25
- S 26
- M 27
- T 28 ●

March
- W 1
- T 2
- F 3
- S 4
- S 5
- M 6 ☽
- T 7
- W 8
- T 9
- F 10
- S 11
- S 12
- M 13 ☺
- T 14
- W 15 ☺
- T 16
- F 17
- S 18
- S 19
- M 20
- T 21
- W 22 ☾
- T 23
- F 24
- S 25
- S 26
- M 27
- T 28
- W 29 ●
- T 30
- F 31

April
- S 1
- S 2
- M 3
- T 4
- W 5 ☽
- T 6
- F 7
- S 8
- S 9
- M 10
- T 11
- W 12
- T 13 ☺
- F 14
- S 15
- S 16
- M 17
- T 18
- W 19
- T 20
- F 21 ☾
- S 22
- S 23
- M 24
- T 25
- W 26
- T 27 ●
- F 28
- S 29
- S 30

May
- M 1
- T 2
- W 3
- T 4
- F 5 ☽
- S 6
- S 7
- M 8
- T 9
- W 10
- T 11
- F 12
- S 13 ☺
- S 14
- M 15
- T 16
- W 17
- T 18
- F 19
- S 20 ☾
- S 21
- M 22
- T 23
- W 24
- T 25
- F 26 ●
- S 27
- S 28
- M 29
- T 30
- W 31

June
- T 1
- F 2
- S 3
- S 4 ☽
- M 5
- T 6
- W 7
- T 8
- F 9
- S 10
- S 11 ☺
- M 12
- T 13
- W 14
- T 15
- F 16
- S 17
- S 18 ☾
- M 19
- T 20
- W 21
- T 22
- F 23
- S 24
- S 25 ●
- M 26
- T 27
- W 28
- T 29
- F 30

2006

July	August	September	October	November	December
S 1	T 1	F 1	S 1	W 1	F 1
S 2	W 2 ☽	S 2		T 2	S 2
	T 3	S 3	M 2	F 3	S 3
M 3 ☽	F 4		T 3	S 4	
T 4	S 5	M 4	W 4	S 5 ☺	M 4
W 5	S 6	T 5	T 5		T 5 ☺
T 6		W 6	F 6	M 6	W 6
F 7	M 7	T 7 ☺	S 7 ☺	T 7	T 7
S 8	T 8	F 8	S 8	W 8	F 8
S 9	W 9 ☺	S 9		T 9	S 9
	T 10	S 10	M 9	F 10	S 10
M 10	F 11		T 10	S 11	
T 11 ☺	S 12	M 11	W 11	S 12 ☾	M 11
W 12	S 13	T 12	T 12		T 12 ☾
T 13		W 13	F 13	M 13	W 13
F 14	M 14	T 14 ☾	S 14 ☾	T 14	T 14
S 15	T 15	F 15	S 15	W 15	F 15
S 16	W 16 ☾	S 16		T 16	S 16
	T 17	S 17	M 16	F 17	S 17
M 17 ☾	F 18		T 17	S 18	
T 18	S 19	M 18	W 18	S 19	M 18
W 19	S 20	T 19	T 19		T 19
T 20		W 20	F 20	M 20 ☺	W 20 ☺
F 21	M 21	T 21	S 21	T 21	T 21
S 22	T 22	F 22 ☺	S 22 ☺	W 22	F 22
S 23	W 23 ☺	S 23		T 23	S 23
	T 24	S 24	M 23	F 24	S 24
M 24	F 25		T 24	S 25	
T 25 ☺	S 26	M 25	W 25	S 26	M 25
W 26	S 27	T 26	T 26		T 26
T 27		W 27	F 27	M 27	W 27 ☽
F 28	M 28	T 28	S 28	T 28 ☽	T 28
S 29	T 29	F 29	S 29 ☽	W 29	F 29
S 30	W 30	S 30 ☽		T 30	S 30
	T 31 ☽		M 30		S 31
M 31			T 31		

2007

January	February	March	April	May	June
M 1	T 1	T 1	S 1	T 1	F 1 ☺
T 2	F 2 ☺	F 2	—	W 2 ☺	S 2
W 3 ☺	S 3	S 3	M 2 ☺	T 3	S 3
T 4	S 4	S 4 ☺	T 3	F 4	—
F 5	—	—	W 4	S 5	M 4
S 6	M 5	M 5	T 5	S 6	T 5
S 7	T 6	T 6	F 6	—	W 6
—	W 7	W 7	S 7	M 7	T 7
M 8	T 8	T 8	S 8	T 8	F 8 (
T 9	F 9	F 9	—	W 9	S 9
W 10	S 10 (	S 10	M 9	T 10 (	S 10
T 11 (	S 11	S 11	T 10 (	F 11	—
F 12	—	—	W 11	S 12	M 11
S 13	M 12	M 12 (	T 12	S 13	T 12
S 14	T 13	T 13	F 13	—	W 13
—	W 14	W 14	S 14	M 14	T 14
M 15	T 15	T 15	S 15	T 15	F 15 ●
T 16	F 16	F 16	—	W 16 ●	S 16
W 17	S 17 ●	S 17	M 16	T 17	S 17
T 18	S 18	S 18	T 17 ●	F 18	—
F 19 ●	—	—	W 18	S 19	M 18
S 20	M 19	M 19 ●	T 19	S 20	T 19
S 21	T 20	T 20	F 20	—	W 20
—	W 21	W 21	S 21	M 21	T 21
M 22	T 22	T 22	S 22	T 22	F 22)
T 23	F 23	F 23	—	W 23)	S 23
W 24	S 24)	S 24	M 23	T 24	S 24
T 25	S 25	S 25)	T 24)	F 25	—
F 26)	—	—	W 25	S 26	M 25
S 27	M 26	M 26	T 26	S 27	T 26
S 28	T 27	T 27	F 27	—	W 27
—	W 28	W 28	S 28	M 28	T 28
M 29		T 29	S 29	T 29	F 29
T 30		F 30	—	W 30	S 30 ☺
W 31		S 31	M 30	T 31	

2007

July

S	1
M	2
T	3
W	4
T	5
F	6
S	7 ☾
S	8
M	9
T	10
W	11
T	12
F	13
S	14 ●
S	15
M	16
T	17
W	18
T	19
F	20
S	21
S	22 ☽
M	23
T	24
W	25
T	26
F	27
S	28
S	29
M	30 ○
T	31

August

W	1
T	2
F	3
S	4
S	5 ☾
M	6
T	7
W	8
T	9
F	10
S	11
S	12
M	13 ●
T	14
W	15
T	16
F	17
S	18
S	19
M	20
T	21 ☽
W	22
T	23
F	24
S	25
S	26
M	27
T	28 ○
W	29
T	30
F	31

September

S	1
S	2
M	3
T	4 ☾
W	5
T	6
F	7
S	8
S	9
M	10
T	11 ●
W	12
T	13
F	14
S	15
S	16
M	17
T	18
W	19 ☽
T	20
F	21
S	22
S	23
M	24
T	25
W	26 ○
T	27
F	28
S	29
S	30

October

M	1
T	2
W	3 ☾
T	4
F	5
S	6
S	7
M	8
T	9
W	10
T	11 ●
F	12
S	13
S	14
M	15
T	16
W	17
T	18
F	19 ☽
S	20
S	21
M	22
T	23
W	24
T	25
F	26 ○
S	27
S	28
M	29
T	30
W	31

November

T	1 ☾
F	2
S	3
S	4
M	5
T	6
W	7
T	8
F	9
S	10 ●
S	11
M	12
T	13
W	14
T	15
F	16
S	17 ☽
S	18
M	19
T	20
W	21
T	22
F	23
S	24 ○
S	25
M	26
T	27
W	28
T	29
F	30

December

S	1 ☾
S	2
M	3
T	4
W	5
T	6
F	7
S	8
S	9 ●
M	10
T	11
W	12
T	13
F	14
S	15
S	16
M	17 ☽
T	18
W	19
T	20
F	21
S	22
S	23
M	24 ○
T	25
W	26
T	27
F	28
S	29
S	30
M	31 ☾

2008

January
T	1	♒	
W	2	♒	
T	3	♓	
F	4	♓	
S	5	♈	
S	6	♈	
M	7	♈	
T	8	♉	●
W	9	♉	
T	10	♊	
F	11	♊	
S	12	♋	
S	13	♋	
M	14	♋	
T	15	♌	☽
W	16	♌	
T	17	♍	
F	18	♍	
S	19	♎	
S	20	♎	
M	21	♏	
T	22	♏	☺
W	23	♐	
T	24	♐	
F	25	♑	
S	26	♑	
S	27	♒	
M	28	♒	
T	29	♒	
W	30	♓	☾
T	31	♓	

February
F	1	♈	
S	2	♈	
S	3	♈	
M	4	♉	
T	5	♉	
W	6	♊	
T	7	♊	●
F	8	♊	
S	9	♋	
S	10	♋	
M	11	♌	
T	12	♌	
W	13	♍	
T	14	♍	☽
F	15	♎	
S	16	♎	
S	17	♏	
M	18	♏	
T	19	♐	
W	20	♐	
T	21	♐	☺
F	22	♑	
S	23	♑	
S	24	♒	
M	25	♒	
T	26	♓	
W	27	♓	
T	28	♓	
F	29	♈	☾

March
S	1	♈	
S	2	♈	
M	3	♉	
T	4	♉	
W	5	♊	
T	6	♊	
F	7	♋	●
S	8	♋	
S	9	♋	
M	10	♌	
T	11	♌	
W	12	♍	
T	13	♍	
F	14	♍	☽
S	15	♎	
S	16	♎	
M	17	♏	
T	18	♏	
W	19	♏	
T	20	♐	
F	21	♐	☺
S	22	♑	
S	23	♑	
M	24	♑	
T	25	♒	
W	26	♒	
T	27	♓	
F	28	♓	
S	29	♈	☾
S	30	♈	
M	31	♈	

April
T	1	♉	
W	2	♉	
T	3	♊	
F	4	♊	
S	5	♊	
S	6	♋	●
M	7	♋	
T	8	♌	
W	9	♌	
T	10	♍	
F	11	♍	
S	12	♎	☽
S	13	♎	
M	14	♏	
T	15	♏	
W	16	♐	
T	17	♐	
F	18	♑	
S	19	♑	
S	20	♑	☺
M	21	♒	
T	22	♒	
W	23	♓	
T	24	♓	
F	25	♈	
S	26	♈	
S	27	♈	
M	28	♉	☾
T	29	♉	
W	30	♊	

May
T	1	♋	
F	2	♋	
S	3	♌	
S	4	♌	
M	5	♍	●
T	6	♍	
W	7	♎	
T	8	♎	
F	9	♏	
S	10	♏	
S	11	♏	
M	12	♐	☽
T	13	♐	
W	14	♑	
T	15	♑	
F	16	♒	
S	17	♒	
S	18	♓	
M	19	♓	
T	20	♓	☺
W	21	♈	
T	22	♈	
F	23	♉	
S	24	♉	
S	25	♉	
M	26	♊	
T	27	♊	
W	28	♋	☾
T	29	♋	
F	30	♌	
S	31	♌	

June
S	1	♍	
M	2	♍	
T	3	♎	●
W	4	♎	
T	5	♏	
F	6	♏	
S	7	♐	
S	8	♐	
M	9	♑	
T	10	♑	☽
W	11	♑	
T	12	♒	
F	13	♒	
S	14	♓	
S	15	♓	
M	16	♓	
T	17	♈	
W	18	♈	☺
T	19	♉	
F	20	♉	
S	21	♉	
S	22	♊	
M	23	♊	
T	24	♋	
W	25	♋	
T	26	♋	☾
F	27	♌	
S	28	♌	
S	29	♍	
M	30	♍	

2008

July			August			September			October			November			December		
T	1		F	1	●	M	1		W	1		S	1		M	1	
W	2		S	2		T	2		T	2		S	2		T	2	
T	3	●	S	3		W	3		F	3					W	3	
F	4					T	4		S	4		M	3		T	4	
S	5		M	4		F	5		S	5		T	4		F	5	)
S	6		T	5		S	6					W	5		S	6	
			W	6		S	7	)	M	6		T	6	)	S	7	
M	7		T	7					T	7	)	F	7				
T	8		F	8	)	M	8		W	8		S	8		M	8	
W	9		S	9		T	9		T	9		S	9		T	9	
T	10	)	S	10		W	10		F	10					W	10	
F	11					T	11		S	11		M	10		T	11	
S	12		M	11		F	12		S	12		T	11		F	12	☺
S	13		T	12		S	13					W	12		S	13	
			W	13		S	14		M	13		T	13	☺	S	14	
M	14		T	14					T	14	☺	F	14				
T	15		F	15		M	15	☺	W	15		S	15		M	15	
W	16		S	16	☺	T	16		T	16		S	16		T	16	
T	17		S	17		W	17		F	17					W	17	
F	18	☺				T	18		S	18		M	17		T	18	
S	19		M	18		F	19		S	19		T	18		F	19	(
S	20		T	19		S	20					W	19	(	S	20	
			W	20		S	21		M	20		T	20		S	21	
M	21		T	21					T	21	(	F	21				
T	22		F	22		M	22	(	W	22		S	22		M	22	
W	23		S	23		T	23		T	23		S	23		T	23	
T	24		S	24	(	W	24		F	24					W	24	
F	25	(				T	25		S	25		M	24		T	25	
S	26		M	25		F	26		S	26		T	25		F	26	
S	27		T	26		S	27					W	26		S	27	●
			W	27		S	28		M	27		T	27	●	S	28	
M	28		T	28					T	28		F	28				
T	29		F	29		M	29	●	W	29	●	S	29		M	29	
W	30		S	30	●	T	30		T	30		S	30		T	30	
T	31		S	31					F	31					W	31	

2009

January

Day	Date	Moon
T	1	
F	2	
S	3	
S	4	☽
M	5	
T	6	
W	7	
T	8	
F	9	
S	10	
S	11	☺
M	12	
T	13	
W	14	
T	15	
F	16	
S	17	
S	18	☾
M	19	
T	20	
W	21	
T	22	
F	23	
S	24	
S	25	
M	26	●
T	27	
W	28	
T	29	
F	30	
S	31	

February

Day	Date	Moon
S	1	
M	2	
T	3	☽
W	4	
T	5	
F	6	
S	7	
S	8	
M	9	☺
T	10	
W	11	
T	12	
F	13	
S	14	
S	15	
M	16	☾
T	17	
W	18	
T	19	
F	20	
S	21	
S	22	
M	23	
T	24	
W	25	●
T	26	
F	27	
S	28	

March

Day	Date	Moon
S	1	
M	2	
T	3	☽
W	4	☽
T	5	
F	6	
S	7	
S	8	
M	9	
T	10	
W	11	☺
T	12	
F	13	
S	14	
S	15	
M	16	
T	17	
W	18	☾
T	19	
F	20	
S	21	
S	22	
M	23	
T	24	
W	25	
T	26	●
F	27	
S	28	
S	29	
M	30	
T	31	

April

Day	Date	Moon
W	1	
T	2	☽
F	3	
S	4	
S	5	
M	6	
T	7	
W	8	
T	9	☺
F	10	
S	11	
S	12	
M	13	
T	14	
W	15	
T	16	
F	17	☾
S	18	
S	19	
M	20	
T	21	
W	22	
T	23	
F	24	
S	25	●
S	26	
M	27	
T	28	
W	29	
T	30	

May

Day	Date	Moon
F	1	☽
S	2	
S	3	
M	4	
T	5	
W	6	
T	7	
F	8	
S	9	☺
S	10	
M	11	
T	12	
W	13	
T	14	
F	15	
S	16	
S	17	☾
M	18	
T	19	
W	20	
T	21	
F	22	
S	23	
S	24	●
M	25	
T	26	
W	27	
T	28	
F	29	
S	30	
S	31	☽

June

Day	Date	Moon
M	1	
T	2	
W	3	
T	4	
F	5	
S	6	
S	7	☺
M	8	
T	9	
W	10	
T	11	
F	12	
S	13	
S	14	
M	15	☾
T	16	
W	17	
T	18	
F	19	
S	20	
S	21	
M	22	●
T	23	
W	24	
T	25	
F	26	
S	27	
S	28	
M	29	☽
T	30	

2009

July	August	September	October	November	December
W 1	S 1	T 1	T 1	S 1	T 1
T 2	S 2	W 2	F 2	—	W 2 ☺
F 3	—	T 3	S 3	M 2 ☺	T 3
S 4	M 3	F 4 ☺	S 4 ☺	T 3	F 4
S 5	T 4	S 5	M 5	W 4	S 5
—	W 5	S 6	T 6	T 5	S 6
M 6	T 6 ☺	—	W 7	F 6	—
T 7 ☺	F 7	M 7	T 8	S 7	M 7
W 8	S 8	T 8	F 9	S 8	T 8
T 9	S 9	W 9	S 10	—	W 9 ☾
F 10	—	T 10	S 11 ☾	M 9 ☾	T 10
S 11	M 10	F 11	—	T 10	F 11
S 12	T 11	S 12 ☾	M 12	W 11	S 12
—	W 12	S 13	T 13	T 12	S 13
M 13	T 13 ☾	—	W 14	F 13	—
T 14	F 14	M 14	T 15	S 14	M 14
W 15 ☾	S 15	T 15	F 16	S 15	T 15
T 16	S 16	W 16	S 17	—	W 16 ●
F 17	—	T 17	S 18 ●	M 16 ●	T 17
S 18	M 17	F 18 ●	—	T 17	F 18
S 19	T 18	S 19	M 19	W 18	S 19
—	W 19	S 20	T 20	T 19	S 20
M 20	T 20 ●	—	W 21	F 20	—
T 21	F 21	M 21	T 22	S 21	M 21
W 22 ●	S 22	T 22	F 23	S 22	T 22
T 23	S 23	W 23	S 24	—	W 23
F 24	—	T 24	S 25	M 23	T 24 ☽
S 25	M 24	F 25	—	T 24 ☽	F 25
S 26	T 25	S 26 ☽	M 26 ☽	W 25	S 26
—	W 26	S 27	T 27	T 26	S 27
M 27	T 27 ☽	—	W 28	F 27	—
T 28 ☽	F 28	M 28	T 29	S 28	M 28
W 29	S 29	T 29	F 30	S 29	T 29
T 30	S 30	W 30	S 31	—	W 30
F 31	—			M 30	T 31 ☺
	M 31				

2010

January	February	March	April	May	June
F 1	M 1	M 1	T 1	S 1	T 1
S 2	T 2	T 2	F 2	S 2	W 2
S 3	W 3	W 3	S 3		T 3
	T 4	T 4	S 4	M 3	F 4 ☾
M 4	F 5	F 5		T 4	S 5
T 5	S 6 ☾	S 6	M 5	W 5	S 6
W 6	S 7	S 7 ☾	T 6 ☾	T 6 ☾	
T 7 ☾			W 7	F 7	M 7
F 8	M 8	M 8	T 8	S 8	T 8
S 9	T 9	T 9	F 9	S 9	W 9
S 10	W 10	W 10	S 10		T 10
	T 11	T 11	S 11	M 10	F 11
M 11	F 12	F 12		T 11	S 12 ●
T 12	S 13	S 13	M 12	W 12	S 13
W 13	S 14 ●	S 14	T 13	T 13	
T 14			W 14 ●	F 14 ●	M 14
F 15 ●	M 15 ●	M 15 ●	T 15	S 15	T 15
S 16	T 16	T 16	F 16	S 16	W 16
S 17	W 17	W 17	S 17		T 17
	T 18	T 18	S 18	M 17	F 18
M 18	F 19	F 19		T 18	S 19 ☽
T 19	S 20	S 20	M 19	W 19	S 20
W 20	S 21	S 21	T 20	T 20	
T 21			W 21 ☽	F 21 ☽	M 21
F 22	M 22 ☽	M 22	T 22	S 22	T 22
S 23 ☽	T 23	T 23 ☽	F 23	S 23	W 23
S 24	W 24	W 24	S 24		T 24
	T 25	T 25	S 25	M 24	F 25
M 25	F 26	F 26		T 25	S 26 ☺
T 26	S 27	S 27	M 26	W 26	S 27
W 27	S 28 ☺	S 28	T 27	T 27	
T 28			W 28 ☺	F 28 ☺	M 28
F 29		M 29	T 29	S 29	T 29
S 30 ☺		T 30 ☺	F 30	S 30	W 30
S 31		W 31		M 31	

2010

July	August	September	October	November	December
T 1 ♋	S 1 ♌	W 1 ♓ ☾	F 1 ♒ ☾	M 1 ♈	W 1 ♉
F 2 ♒		T 2 ♈	S 2 ♒	T 2 ♊	T 2 ♉
S 3 ♒	M 2 ♌	F 3 ♈	S 3 ♓	W 3 ♊	F 3 ♋
S 4 ♓ ☾	T 3 ♍ ☾	S 4 ♒		T 4 ♉	S 4 ♋
	W 4 ♍	S 5 ♒	M 4 ♓	F 5 ♉	S 5 ♌ ●
M 5 ♓	T 5 ♈		T 5 ♊	S 6 ♋ ●	
T 6 ♓	F 6 ♈	M 6 ♌	W 6 ♊	S 7 ♋	M 6 ♌
W 7 ♌	S 7 ♒	T 7 ♌	T 7 ♉ ●		T 7 ♍
T 8 ♌	S 8 ♒	W 8 ♊ ●	F 8 ♉	M 8 ♌	W 8 ♍
F 9 ♍		T 9 ♊	S 9 ♋	T 9 ♌	T 9 ♍
S 10 ♍	M 9 ♌	F 10 ♉	S 10 ♋	W 10 ♍	F 10 ♋
S 11 ♒ ●	T 10 ♍ ●	S 11 ♉		T 11 ♍	S 11 ♋
	W 11 ♊	S 12 ♋	M 11 ♌	F 12 ♋	S 12 ♒
M 12 ♒	T 12 ♊		T 12 ♌	S 13 ♋ ☽	
T 13 ♌	F 13 ♉	M 13 ♋	W 13 ♌	S 14 ♋	M 13 ♒ ☽
W 14 ♌	S 14 ♉	T 14 ♌	T 14 ♍ ☽		T 14 ♒
T 15 ♊	S 15 ♉	W 15 ♌ ☽	F 15 ♍	M 15 ♒	W 15 ♒
F 16 ♊		T 16 ♍	S 16 ♋	T 16 ♒	T 16 ♈
S 17 ♉	M 16 ♋ ☽	F 17 ♍	S 17 ♋	W 17 ♈	F 17 ♈
S 18 ♉ ☽	T 17 ♋	S 18 ♍		T 18 ♈	S 18 ♈
	W 18 ♌	S 19 ♋	M 18 ♋	F 19 ♈	S 19 ♈
M 19 ♋	T 19 ♌		T 19 ♒	S 20 ♈	
T 20 ♋	F 20 ♍	M 20 ♋	W 20 ♒	S 21 ♈ ☺	M 20 ♊
W 21 ♌	S 21 ♍	T 21 ♒	T 21 ♒		T 21 ♊ ☺
T 22 ♌	S 22 ♍	W 22 ♒	F 22 ♈	M 22 ♊	W 22 ♋
F 23 ♌		T 23 ♒ ☺	S 23 ♈ ☺	T 23 ♊	T 23 ♋
S 24 ♍	M 23 ♋	F 24 ♈	S 24 ♌	W 24 ♊	F 24 ♍
S 25 ♍	T 24 ♋ ☺	S 25 ♈		T 25 ♋	S 25 ♍
	W 25 ♒	S 26 ♒	M 25 ♌	F 26 ♋	S 26 ♌
M 26 ♋ ☺	T 26 ♒		T 26 ♍	S 27 ♈	
T 27 ♋	F 27 ♒	M 27 ♒	W 27 ♍	S 28 ♈ ☾	M 27 ♌
W 28 ♋	S 28 ♌	T 28 ♒	T 28 ♋		T 28 ♉ ☾
T 29 ♒	S 29 ♌	W 29 ♈	F 29 ♋	M 29 ♌	W 29 ♉
F 30 ♒		T 30 ♈	S 30 ♋ ☾	T 30 ♌	T 30 ♋
S 31 ♌	M 30 ♍		S 31 ♌		F 31 ♋
	T 31 ♍				

.